Gardener, Go Home

Gardener, Go Home

by KEN KRAFT

APPLETON-CENTURY
New York

Affiliate of
MEREDITH PRESS
Des Moines & New York

Library of Congress Catalogue Card Number: 64-12437

Manufactured in the United States of America for Meredith Press

VAN REES PRESS • NEW YORK

This book is for Major General Frank L. Culin, Jr., and his Ella, whose California garden my wife and I have often enjoyed and sometimes exploited.

CONTENTS

Gardener, Go Home

Chapter 1

THE ONLY *SOPHISTICATED* SPORT

BEFORE you get married, Sonny," a senior citizen told me some years ago, "be sure the girl owns a fur coat and already has her appendix out." He didn't say a word about making sure she wasn't a gardener. That I had to find out for myself, and I found it out when we took a vacation trip the summer after our wedding. On it we happened to go through Springfield, Illinois, and, by George, they were having the state fair there.

"Oh, do let's drop in for a minute," my young wife said. We did, and were there for most of two mortal days, and we knew every prize pumpkin, roasting ear, and beefsteak tomato on sight by the time they closed the fair and ran us out. For, it appeared, my girl had been a tiny gardener in her childhood—and at the sight of such riches again, all the old yearning came tumbling back.

Now, it is possible to find yourself married to a gardener, and not garden. I have known several such people, poor vacant souls. If they overhear you saying "mulch,"

or "tilth," they think your nose must be stuffy. The tips
of their fingernails always have that pathetic white look.
And the nice summer weekends they have to mope away
on smooth green golf courses and at poolside bars with
other miserable non-gardening wretches. As it was, I
would as soon have played beanbag as golf, and so I
became a gardener.

There is an old Chinese saying that ends up: "If you
would be happy for a lifetime, plant a garden." I'm afraid
the translator was confused. "If you would be *busy* for a
lifetime," yes. For gardeners are the least idle of people.
(Did you ever see a gardener lounging in a garden chair?
Neither did I.) This trait makes gardeners awkward visitors—or jewels, depending on how you feel about it when
a nice clean guest suddenly squats at the pansy border to
root out weeds you'd hoped nobody would notice.

In this country alone there are supposed to be about
thirty million home gardeners, which would make gardening the most popular pastime. Hunting and fishing
claim first place with an estimated forty million fans,
but—you notice they have to lump them to make it?
Well, there are plenty of fishermen who would shoot
their toes off if they ever fooled with a musket, and
hunters who can't tell a sinker from a snapping turtle,
so you *can't* lump them.

On the other hand, some hard losers cry that gardening
isn't a pastime at all, for Lord's sake, or any recreation
either, and certainly no sport. There is something to this.
A golfer kisses his wife good-bye and says, "I'm off to play

eighteen holes." "So go," she perhaps says, "for I'm going to play tennis." Or play bridge, or play double bingo, or play shuffleboard. But did you ever in your life hear a gardener say: "Well, I'm off to play hoe," or "I think today I'll play potato bugs"?

The blunt truth is, when a gardener goes out to the garden, he goes out to work. He doesn't pretend he is going to do anything else, either. His business he may call the retail game or the engineering game, but his pastime he calls work. This is what sets us gardeners apart. Ours is the only truly sophisticated sport. We are the adults in the pastime world of grown-up children, for we work, and we say we work, and so we have none of the secret feelings of guilt that come from wasting time instead of working.

In fact, we are so free of guilt feelings, we can be pills to have around. More than one non-gardener has taken up gardening so that he, too, could smell up the neighborhood with fish-oil fertilizer or lime-sulphur spray, and be lordly about the biggest dahlia.

Also, non-gardeners (our kiss-off term, by the way, for devotees of absolutely all other pastimes) are usually only consumers, but we are producers. And if you think this isn't a club, watch a trout fisherman squirm when we ask him how much per pound his fishies cost him, or a golfer trying to brazen out the hideous expense of *his* foolishness. "So you raised a hundred dollars' worth of squashes last summer," such persons will sometimes bawl. "Who would ever in his right senses *buy* a hundred dollars' worth of squashes?" Or roses, sunflowers, horseradish . . .

The answer to this caterwauling is a firm and dignified: "*I* would," and all that the non-gardener can do is to grow tenser and guiltier, and turn splotchy. It makes up for all the blisters and calluses, and the bushels of tiresome squashes we quietly bury in the compost bin every August.

Chapter 2

GARDENER AGAINST THE WORLD

W HAT'S all this talk about gardening making people tolerant? You show me a gardener who is tolerant, let's say when he shucks an ear of his home-grown sweet corn and finds a borer staring out at him, and I'll show you a gardener who is out of his mind. If rational, he'll dance with rage on the borer, bay at the sky, and switch brands of bug doom for the sixth time that summer.

This should surprise no one. Compared to other sports, gardening is simply bristling with enemies. A golfer may have a trifling little trouble with cross winds or with a tree or two growing where his ball wants to go; and fishermen get their lines snarled, probably through fool carelessness; and hunters occasionally mistake each other for moose; but gardeners—!

Not even counting such villains as the weatherman (who will be hissed separately), gardeners are beset by birds, bugs, dogs, chickens, deer, moles, cats, rats, mice, rabbits, people with big feet, wild hogs, raccoons, termite exterminators, elephants,[1] utility men, gophers, and visitors who say how odd that all their other friends' gardens are doing so much better. This is only a partial list. No gardener has ever had the heart to make a complete one, and nobody would believe him anyway.

Gardeners have so many troubles that they are even trouble to each other. When you see a gardener dashing out of the house in the middle of winter and gnashing his teeth in the snow, he has very likely just heard from friends in California reporting that the pelargoniums and fuchsias are blooming their heads off, and mercy, what a chore keeping the oranges picked. Incidentally, this explains California's population explosion: it's frozen people going there to write their own letters.

When they arrive, they find the orange pickers didn't mention the deer and gophers. California deer get so casual during the closed season, gardeners have to weed around them, or do their gardening inside cages. Gophers can burrow under the cages. They aren't satisfied with grubs, as are moles, but are crazy about roots.[2] And California birds are worse than other birds about eating gar-

[1] In Africa and India and occasionally in the neighborhood of happy-go-lucky zoos and circuses in the United States. Elephants enjoy yanking turnips right out of the ground.

[2] A gopher harvests a beet, for instance, by pulling it down into his run. The face of a gardener seeing his row of beets disappearing into the ground feet first is a scream, if it's somebody else. One gentleman in La Canada, California, was loafing on his patio smiling at his prize gladiolus one minute and at a hole in the ground the next. Yep, gophers again.

den sass. However, Californians don't get much sympathy for their troubles from the rest of the country.

If any dog has made a name for himself as a friend of the garden, it has escaped my attention, and cats are not much better. If they do happen to catch a field mouse or a mole, there's no living with them, and they parade it through the whole house when you have company. The best thing a gardener can say for cats is that they aren't vegetarians. A St. Louis gardener reported that a neighborhood tomcat went around snapping off tulip blooms with his paws, but he didn't eat them, so it doesn't count. I once knew a dog that ate tomatoes, but I think he was taken in by the color.

Not all insects are in bad with gardeners; bees, for instance. Most spiders are on our side too.[3] Also ladybugs and praying mantises. (Or "mantes." The dictionary prefers it, but it sounds like something you'd wear, doesn't it?) Expecting the average gardener to sort out the good insects from the bad ones is like expecting the average girl to be nice to useful snakes. To your average gardener, "goddamn'bugs" is all one word.

Since chickens are no longer the back-yard enterprise they once were, city gardeners have ceased to feel strongly

[3] Strictly speaking, they are arachnids, not insects. Spiders don't care what you call them but entomologists are sticklers for form. Scorpions, mites, and ticks are also arachnids, bad luck to them.

about them. Younger gardeners don't even know what you're talking about. A man in Wilderville, Oregon, found that chickens in the garden were nothing compared to peacocks. His pet peacock pulled every radish as fast as it reached eating size, and the peacock didn't even care for radishes. He laid them down in neat ranks like dominoes.

To a hunter a wild hog is an opportunity, but to a rural gardener it's a disaster. Hunters call tame hogs that have gone native feral hogs. Gardeners call them whatever comes fiercely to mind. Hogs damage a garden by rooting, the hog equivalent of raus mit 'em. A hog-rooted garden looks like an exploded mattress. It does save plowing for the replanting, but don't tell that to a hog-disturbed gardener and expect him to shake hands with you.

Raccoons are not as violent as wild hogs, but there are more of them, and they eat, eat, eat. They aren't as wild as wild hogs, either, and some people get them to drop around for tidbits on the kitchen doorstep in the evening, as conversation pieces. They sometimes inflict a mean bite on the hand feeding them, a thing gardeners regard as poetic justice, and no wonder. One summer my wife spent six weeks waking up several times every night and shining a flashlight out the window at a raccoon family that was gradually stripping a peach tree growing alongside the house. In the end she got a handful of peaches and bags under her eyes. Some people tie rags and tin cans on trees to alarm raccoons. This would work if raccoons had a sense of humor, as they would probably die laughing, but they don't have one. A man in Atlanta tied a lifelike dummy in his cherry tree, and the neighbors thought he had hung himself. The raccoons stole his cherries just the same, and also a package of peppermints in the dummy's coat pocket.

Some gardeners consider termite exterminators worse than both raccoons and wild hogs put together and would sell the house at a loss sooner than go through it again. The termite men deny they squirt oil on shrubs and stomp flower borders and throw wormy timbers into fishpools on purpose. They say it is just that their minds are entirely on business, and after all, what are they there for? This is something like being asked to be grateful to a mule for kicking you out of the way of a drunken driver; you'd almost rather take your chances.

As to utility men, the main kick gardeners have against them is as to where they plant their poles. The utility men say there is no way to keep a gardener happy (and secretly, they think their poles are rather pretty) . Some gardeners try to take the curse off a pole spang in the middle of the lawn by running vines up it, or hanging bird houses and mosquito torches on it. This is frowned on by the men who have to climb the pole with the gardener standing there watching.

The time to do something about a utility pole is while the utility men are making up their minds where to put it. A Kentucky gardener made the discovery that she was able to control the placement of a pole by the simplest of devices—she had a hunch that if she put in a bed of chrysanthemums at a certain spot, that would do it. It certainly did. The utility boys came charging in and began digging their pole hole in the center of the bed. They didn't realize until too late that she had not taken the chrysanthemums out of their pots, and was able to whisk them off to another bed which had been skillfully disguised as a pile of leaves.

A Missouri gardener who had a little lake on a weekend place in the country discovered to his horror that the telephone he had just ordered was going to need a pole for its line exactly in the middle of the lake's nice grassy dam. While nobody was looking, he yanked out the stake which marked this spot, and stabbed it into a place right in the lake—six feet from the shore on one side, where an elm tree would hide anything from view of the house. When the pole crew arrived, laughing and scratching, in went the pole where the stake now was, in two feet of water and no questions asked. It has been handy to tie a skiff to ever since.

Chapter 3

AH, THE PROUD GARDENER

ONE of the things that turn supermarket managers psychotic before their time is home gardeners. I mean vegetable gardeners. "Here I am, having a pretty good day," a supermarket manager told me. "Maybe I'm whistling, even. Nobody's swiped a shopping cart this morning, or collapsed the canned pineapple pyramid display—like on their kid's head. Then all of a sudden I see one of them fiendishly weighing up a pound of peas, and my day is ruined, that's all, ruined."

By "one of them" he referred to a customer with a home vegetable patch, intent on an odious comparison. I knew precisely what he meant, because I—well, I didn't tell him *how* I knew. But I can see it now: the man and wife sauntering along the supermarket aisle, the husband's eyes glittering as he spots a bin of peas. He pounces, snatches up handfuls of peas and dribbles them on the scale's pan until the hand of the scale is exactly on sixteen ounces. Just as the manager, peeking from that little spy hole they always have in their tiny office, is rubbing his hands over the sale, the customer shows his wife the pound of peas, laughing harshly.

"Look what you get soaked thirty-three cents for," he trumpets, jerking heads up all over the store. "Why, I dump better peas than these in the compost!" He flings them back into the bin and starts darting around to see what else they're robbing the public with this morning. This is very rough on pea sales as well as on the supermarket manager's family when he comes dragging home at the end of the day. And if his wife happens to be a vegetable gardener herself—well! Here we go all over again.

The same situation seldom prevails with florists *versus* home flower gardeners. For some reason, flower gardeners are more modest about their accomplishments. They can look at a carnation in a florist's window without slapping their legs and bursting into coarse laughter. Some of them even loosen up and buy a nosegay once in a while without making a thing of trying to figure out how many potential dollars are blooming in their yards. To a vegetable gardener, this isn't playing the game. Privately, every vegetable gardener thinks every flower gardener just doesn't know what it's all about, and probably was dropped on his head in a potato bin when young.[1]

---

[1] Do I hear a question asking "What about gardeners who raise both vegetables *and* flowers?" Well, if you ask them, they'll tell you they are persons of vision and broad appreciation. Ac-

All vegetable gardeners dream of some day keeping absolutely perfect track of the true market value of their produce throughout an entire season. None ever has, but it would make an accountant giddy to watch some of them trying to. I know a man who asked his wife to keep such a running account one summer of how much they got out of their little back-yard vegetable garden, so he could square with his conscience the $17.50 he had blown for seeds, tools, and whatnot. His wife turned out to be a person of iron moral standards, and to his dismay he found she was chalking up the score in such piddling amounts as:

Beans for dinner....................	3 cents
Parsley for Sunday roast garnish.....	½ cent
Four carrots (pretty small).........	2½ cents

At this rate he felt it would take him three growing seasons to make back the nut, but she said right was right, and she didn't hold with loose round numbers. Still, the story had a sort of happy ending. Even with such tight-fisted figuring, the man came out with a forty-dollar profit on the garden if he didn't count their time. His wife insisted on counting their time, and was arguing that the garden still owed them $710 by the time a killing frost put a stop to the whole business.

---

cording to flower gardeners, they're misguided. According to vegetable gardeners, they're wishy-washy. Let's be kind and just call them schizophrenic.

Even though vegetable gardeners and flower gardeners travel different roads on dollar-pride in their efforts, they split right down the middle when it comes to seed buyers compared with plant buyers. The good-natured contempt with which a vegetable or flower gardener who grows everything from seed regards one who buys plants is discouraging to people who think this world will have peace when we ban the bomb. Furthermore, this seeders-against-planters thing is a lopsided commotion. All the action is on the side of the seeders, like a wave of motor-bike riders curling their lips at the plump family sedans they are zizzing past on a Sunday afternoon. When a plant buyer does catch on, he is apt to make the mistake of being apologetic. You will overhear conversations like this, say, between utter strangers during an intermission:

"Good show, what?"

"Fair, but the playwright's sure no gardener. Planting those tomatoes under that tree!"

"Righto. Gardener myself. Love tomatoes."

"So? Try that new Astronaut Hybrid yet? *There's* a tomato!"

"Good. I'll buy some plants, and . . ."

"*Plants!* Did you say . . . *plants?*"

"Why—er—"

"You have to *grow* 'em, mister. From *seed.*"

"From . . .?"

"Seed, seed! You know what seeds are, don't you?"

"Oh—seeds. Say—maybe if I got some of this—er—seed, and asked the nursery to raise me some plants . . .

Sir! Sir! Please don't rush off like that. I didn't mean any harm. . . ."[2]

[2] Now and then a plant buyer will protest that he has room in his garden for only a few things, and if he bought seed he'd get hundreds more plants than he could use. This kind of talk gets hollow cackles from seeders, who know more than they're admitting about d-mp-ng -ff.

Chapter 4

ARDEN-GAY ATIN-LAY

S PEAKING of cleavages between gardeners, the Grand Canyon of them all is the one that separates the botanical-name users from the other, or Who-say-dat? school. Try to tell a little old lady gardener that her pet snowball bush is really *Viburnum tomentosum plicatum,* and she'll ruffle up and squawk all over you. And she'd be right, in a way. Calling her snowball by its Latin name makes it sound to her a stranger, and a stranger she wouldn't ask in to tea.

That's one of the kicks against botanical names—the noise so many of them make on the ear, compared to poetic common names. For example:

Love-lies-bleeding is *Amaranthus caudatus.*
Swan River daisy is *Brachycome iberidifolia.*
Farewell-to-spring is *Godetia amoena.*
Love-in-a-mist is *Nigella damascena.*
And so on.

To this the botanical-name people have a pat answer: "Common names vary from place to place, but botanical

18

ones, never." Not everyone adores consistency, of course, but this isn't much of a rebuttal.[1]

"Botanical names are like good manners," said one gardener in a calling-the-meeting-to-order voice. "You can always tell which persons were brought up on them, from the ones who were calling *Dicentra spectablis* 'bleeding heart' until day before yesterday." This seems a stony attitude, slamming the door on self-improvement. A kinder and more perceptive point of view is this one, by a gardener who keeps her ears open:

"It makes no difference how long you've used botanical names—the important thing is why you use them," said she. "Are you trying to impress somebody, or are you simply interested in being exact?" Well, that nails it down. And if you're trying to impress somebody, Lord save you from an uncomplicated soul who doesn't impress, such as a man I know who asked for the name of a certain flower of a woman who had been cowing her friends for years with glib garden Latin.

Instead of saying "false dragonhead," which would have satisfied him, she had to rattle off her own version of the botanical name. He didn't catch it, and she repeated it, a bit faster. He still didn't get it. She began to fidget. "All I can make out is 'footsie,'" he said, mystified. "Isn't there more to it than that?" No, there

---

[1] A better one would be: Botanical names do so vary, sometimes. This can happen when more than one botanist names the same plant. From then on the poor thing is saddled with the alternate name(s) in parentheses.

wasn't, she said, rather snappily, so he asked her to spell it. That floored her completely. He finally had to go off and sleuth it out at the public library for himself. Next time they met, he pinned her down: "It's *Phy-so-ste-gia,*" he told her in a loud, clear, triumphant voice in front of everybody. "Full name: *Physostegia virginia.*" She has never been quite the same since then, poor dear.

Another hazard is the terribly basic-minded type of non-gardener. He wants to know not only what the botanical name is, but what it means, if you please. Should you be so foolish as to call a lilac *Syringa vulgaris* in front of him, you're in for it. You can bluff out *vulgaris*, but then what? "Does *Syringa* mean like a syringe?" he'll inquire. "Squirting like? Who ever saw a lilac squirting?" The best thing is to suggest he look it up for himself, and incidentally tell you the answer. He'll do it anyway, and you'll get credit for honest ignorance.[2]

Unless you're very lucky, he'll also want you to break any botanical name into pieces: "What's that first part? The model, or the breed, or what?" Tell him it's the genus, and you deserve your fate. You'll end up tracing the thing from strains, through varieties, and so on up to the very vegetable kingdom itself, if you are able. If you're like most of us, you'll change the subject.

[2] If anybody's dying to know, it is taken from the Greek by way of Neo-Latin and is a modification of the word for pipe: syrinx. They were thinking of pipe as in Pan, not Dunhill.

Probably the worst effects of the botanical-versus-common nomenclature come when it rends asunder man and wife. In the vast majority of cases it is the woman who becomes converted to botanical naming and brings this about. From then on she is more a mystery than ever to her husband, and at times a real blister. Even if she doesn't try to drag him into the true faith with her, she continues to be a pain in the ear to him, and usually there is nothing he can do about it. Not always, though. There is at least one case on file where the husband proved pretty spry himself.

His wife had joined a garden club two years before, and things had gradually got so that when he and she were outdoors he might as well have been strolling with Mark Antony. He couldn't understand two words out of every three she spoke. It was *dissitiflora* this and *variegata* that until he was dizzy, and he thought her cooking was suffering, too. But he was much too professional a husband to think he could get anywhere by asking her to be reasonable.

Instead, he decided to fight fire with fire. He slyly began book-learning on, mainly, vegetables, his own particular garden interest. He sprang it on his wife a week or so later by remarking casually that the *Brassica oleracea* was doing nicely. "Oh?" said his wife, looking blankly at the broccoli he was talking about.

"Yes," he said smoothly, "though it isn't as thrifty as my *Apium graveolens* . . . or don't you agree?"

"Why, uh—" she said, watching from the corner of

her eye to try and catch him looking at what on earth he was talking about.

Instead of telling her it was plain old celery, he moved gaily on to the lettuce bed. "We'd better use up this *Lactuca sativa* before it bolts," he observed. "Warm weather now."

"Lettuce?" his wife said quickly. "Yes, yes . . ."

"And that means it's about time to plant *Hibiscus esculentus*," he added.

"Hibiscus?" his wife cried, finally feeling herself on familiar ground. "In the vegetable garden, for pity's sake . . . ?"

"Apparently you didn't catch the species name, my dear," he said kindly. "*Esculentus*. Latin, of course, for 'good to eat.' "

"Good to eat?" she mumbled.

"Okra, to be sure," he said, and added that it was Asiatic in origin. She said something about having to go do something in the house, but he detained her a few more moments. "You might take along *Petroselinum hortense*," he said, stopping beside the parsley bed.

"Hortense?" she cried, grasping at straws. "Hortense who?"

He handed her a bunch of parsley and patted her cheek. "You wanted her to garnish the roast, I believe, my pet. By the way, did you know this was one of the plants grown in Charlemagne's garden?" The poor ignorant wretch didn't know, of course, any more than a possum. "Though *Allium cepa* is still older," he went on.

"One of the oldest of cultivated plants. But *Allium porrum* is said to date back even farther, back to prehistoric times." He looked at her. "Imagine that!"

She swallowed hard. "John," she said meekly, "I haven't any idea what you're talking about."

"Why, merely onions and leeks, my dear," he said.

"Oh," she said, and after a brief silence she crept into the house. When he followed a few minutes later, she was arranging a bouquet. "Dinner will be ready in a few minutes, John," she remarked, "as soon as I finish with this *Scabiosa* . . ." she pulled up short. ". . . this mourning-bride bouquet."

He started measuring out gin for a martini. "*Scabiosa atropurpurea grandiflora*," he murmured. She looked up, their eyes met, and they both laughed out loud till they were weak. They've been terribly well adjusted ever since.[3]

[3] When pronounced wrongly, with a short "a," *Scabiosa* sounds pretty punk. The word traces back to Medieval Latin, meaning a cure for scabies. Scabies is a general term for some skin diseases of sheep, cattle, and man, and some plants in the genus *Scabiosa* were said to cure scabies. How we got from there to "mourning bride" is a wonder.

Chapter 5

HAPPINESS IS A WARM COMPOST

ASIDE from its convenience as a catch-all, the compost pile is a neutral ground on which organic gardeners can meet non-organic ones.[1] Anybody who knows any organic gardeners knows there are precious few such neutral grounds, too. But the compost pile is the most enduring hope for humus for all of us, so composting gets to be terribly serious business. You can easily check this for yourself every time any of us sticks a spade into our ripe compost and hefts a scoop of blackish crunchy stuff. See the joy on our faces as we jiggle it off into a wheelbarrow as if panning for gold, sorting out the old chicken bones and a mossy teaspoon Mother has been turning the house upside down hunting for these past weeks. This is the kind of thing money can't buy.

The very first compost pile my wife and I built was

[1] Well, fairly neutral. Non-organic gardeners may add chemicals to hurry it along. Compost feels it has all the time in the world.

pure organic-garden, though somewhat by chance. It just happened that we landed in a house in Arlington, Virginia, next door to an elderly Dutch couple, who were mostly organic gardeners. That is, they used a little chemical fertilizer, but apologetically. When we took it into our heads to plant a few peas, these neighbors eagerly gave us the word—manure, if you could get it, which you couldn't, and compost, and *ach*, those fine earthworms. We were instantly converted, and like converts to other religions, boned up on the subject and grew so stern and pure that we shortly had the charter members chewing their nails.

"You're not going to build your compost pile there?" they had cried when they saw us digging a spade-deep hole six feet long and three wide under a willow tree near the fence line. "It will feed that *Dummkopf* tree!" It seemed they had been praying for years that lightning would hit the willow, which shaded their garden.

We said we were sorry, but this was the only possible spot in the yard for a compost pile—superior drainage, erosion-protected, thermally balanced, bacterially dynamic. They stood blinking across the fence at us, and later we noticed them whispering over their own compost pile, located where the bottom had dropped out of a bagful of garbage one time.

When we had our pile built three feet high in layers (shredded vegetable matter, lime, earth; shredded vegetable matter, lime, earth . . .) with steeply sloping sides and a concave top, I borrowed a crowbar from our neighbors and bored several shafts in the pile after careful measuring. From a series of little packets I then poured various herblike stuffs into the holes, plugged them with earth, and watered the whole thing. "Catalysts, you know," I remarked to the husband, who had been watching the rite from the corner of his eye. "We sent off for them."

"Please . . . what they are?" he asked after a half-minute struggle with himself.

"I don't really know," I said in truth. He regarded me sadly, plainly convinced I knew exactly and had probably invented them. To this day I don't know, but our compost pile made compost about as good as that from our neighbors' pile, which was shaped like a derby hat and whistled on warm days.

Another school of composters claims you need an earth-floored wooden bin to make it in. A splinter group says to make the bin of concrete, and another says you don't need an earth floor at all and in fact can use an old barrel, blending the compost by rolling the barrel downhill on weekends. Most composters frown on such labor-saving gimmicks, holding that the sweat that runs down the spade handle is the secret ingredient.[2]

We have never built a compost bin, but we know quite

[2] The indispensable ingredient is, or are, bacteria. Bacteria have been on earth longer than any other form of life, and, like people, there are good bacteria and bad ones. Some of the good ones change raw materials into forms plants can feed on (as nitrogen into nitrate, sulphur into sulphate).

a bit about two of them. They were side by side in the service court of a house we were about to lease, and at first glance I mistook them for the garage. "Garage is over there," my wife said, pointing to it. "Those other things must be the pony stables. Or maybe they breed Great Danes."

The owner of the house suddenly appeared and cleared matters up. She seized the edge of the roof of one stable and thrust it upward. "These are my wonderful compost bins, ee—e—e—e," she said, letting the lid slam down and blowing us backward with the wind. Her haste was due to a field rat that was shopping around in the compost. It was a great attraction for them; they doted on the colored paper napkins that occasionally arrived, and they built delicate nests, like wee Easter baskets, with them. This did nothing at all to endear them to the owner, a lady scientist named Maud.

Maud slammed almost everything except old rubber tires into her compost bins, as if they were incinerators, and seldom chopped the stuff up first, either, but she got good compost just the same, in time.[3]

Also, when Maud's compost was ready to use, you didn't have to buy seeds—you could plant the compost

[3] You never know what you'll find in a compost pile. Most gardeners omit absolutely non-organic things such as teacups, but this still leaves a lot of room for experiment. Among the odd things composted from time to time have been straw hats, gift cigars, neighbors' cats, trashy novels, unsuccessful casseroles, and bedroom slippers. Compared to a compost pile, the inside of a woman's handbag is tidy.

and get a free thrill waiting to see what came up. In this way we eventually wallowed in tomatoes galore, lemon sprouts, apple sprouts, melon vines, potatoes, avocado sprouts, garlic, and corn. The bins had cost $150 to build and could have carried an amusement tax.

Speaking of costs, the most expensive compost on record was some that a lady organic gardener created in her back yard in San Francisco. Her house was ninety years old, and though it was of wood it had escaped the great fire of 1906 and was doing nicely until the compost came along. One day a carpenter was poking around, and he came charging out from between the joists dotted with bugs. "Nonsense, I don't permit bugs," the owner said when he showed her.

Just then there was a dull rumble below, and the floor sagged. "Run for your life!" the carpenter howled. "The place is riddled." Seems the compost had attracted termites, and the termites got into the house, the lady having had the bad luck to build her pile smack against the foundation. After paying for the repairs she estimated the compost was worth $17.88 a tablespoon, and she rushed right out and bought a garbage grinder for her sink and canceled her subscription to *Bio-Dynamics*.

Chapter 6

HOTBEDS, COLD-FRAMES, AND
NERVOUS PROSTRATION

A HOTBED has been called the poor man's green-house, and I suppose the one who called it that was a poor man who had followed to the letter some of the instructions you can find in garden books for building the hotbed beautiful. In fact, I know such a poor man. During the time he was on this hotbed kick he became a horrible example to all his friends, none of whom has touched a hotbed with a ten-foot pole since.

For one thing, he read up on the subject so well beforehand that he became a misery to have around. Ask him to have a quick drink with you at five o'clock and you'd get a lecture with it: "Old boy, do you realize that, basically, hotbeds and cold-frames are identical in construction?" he would say with the air of a lawyer telling you you were sole heir to the Mississippi Bubble. If you weren't awfully careful, he would buy a second round to keep you from escaping while he drew pictures on a bar napkin to show the proper arrangement of the heating cable in the hotbed ideal. "And sixty running feet provides bottom heat for thirty-six square feet of frame. Isn't that interesting?"

He was such a nice fellow when he wasn't on hotbeds that nobody wanted to hurt his feelings. As an optimist in the crowd once said, while munching a potato chip, "Let's just be thankful he doesn't heat the damn thing with horse manure."

In all fairness it should be said that our hotbed enthusiast did not, at least, try to make it sound easy. I hate to think how many suburban husbands show up at the office Monday morning holding one hand to their backs and making faces because they took too literally such instructions as: "The advantage of a hotbed or cold-frame is that it is easily moved. Simply pick it up and set it in any advantageous spot, such as over a bed of plants you wish to protect when cold weather approaches." The trouble with this kind of directions is that the gardener thinks they are talking to him. They aren't. They are talking to two strong men, a couple of boys to get in the way, and a woman to tell them why it'll never work.

Speaking of women, there is nothing like cold-frames and hotbeds to separate the girls from the boys. If you see a frame thrown together slapdash and perhaps with a strong list to leeward, you can be pretty sure a woman gardener made it. When a man builds a frame he is likely to go about it as though he planned to live in the thing and he uses chalk line, spirit level, square, and drill. Occasionally a man will make a frame of brick or rock, for more permanence, something a woman would never dream of doing. Her idea is: never mind what it looks like—get it going.[1]

A woman gardener I know once asked her husband to make her a hotbed, and regretted it almost at once. She asked him on a Saturday morning, supposing he would have it ready by noon. By noon he had merely mulled over all the scrap lumber he had on hand, and had gone off to inquire at a builders' supply house for two-inch planks of chestnut. He said he would take cypress if he had to, but he much preferred chestnut. And he specified heartwood, too. Redwood was the only thing they had on hand that would do at all, so he said he would have to have hot-dipped galvanized screws, to avoid corrosion in the years to come.[2]

By this time his wife was growing restless, as it was getting on toward three o'clock, and she wanted to plant a few things in her new hotbed before dark. Her husband said a job worth doing was worth doing well, and thought he might possibly finish the hotbed the next day, barring unexpected problems.

[1] Both sexes are interested in results, but women are better at it.

[2] If he had used wood treated for decay with pentachlorophenol, its toxic fumes would have hurt the plants. Pronouncing pentachlorophenol is one of the hazards of gardening. Mercury and creosote compounds as wood preservatives are just as hard on plants and much easier to say.

Well, to wrap the story up, by the end of the following week, he had produced a beautiful hotbed in his basement workshop, all sanded and varnished, made to fit exactly a standard-size sash, a point he had carefully checked beforehand, and with brass plug-in fittings and a weatherproof switch on one end, for the heating cable. He went to look up his wife to ask her where she wanted the hotbed placed. When he found her she was already planting her plants inside a drunken circle she had made out of some ten-inch strips of linoleum left over from the kitchen floor, with a sixty-watt bulb on an extension cord from the garage for heat and an old shower curtain weighted down with rocks for a sash. Her husband stopped speaking to her for a while, and it was just as well, since he discovered that the basement door opening was the one thing he had forgotten to measure during the project, and to get the new redwood hotbed frame outside, he had to kick it to pieces.

Hotbeds and cold-frames have, in fact, been responsible for quite a lot of domestic bickering, mostly over the ventilation. It is a rare thing for husband and wife to agree on how much ventilation a frame needs. Husbands who insist on sleeping with the bedroom window wide open in wintertime seem apt to take an opposite view when it comes to a frame, while wives who could sleep in a clothes closet are always flinging the frame sash up. The result is that several times a winter the poor fellow will find himself being shaken by the shoulder just as he finally gets to sleep, and told, "Darling, I just remembered—the frame is open, and it's supposed to go below freezing tonight." The best advice for people such as this is: sleep in a ground-floor room that has a window on the south side, put the frame right under the window in easy reach from inside, and count to ten before replying to any remarks made after midnight.[3]

[3] Or ventilation may be made automatic for hotbeds by the use of thermostatically operated devices. A small boy and a baseball can ventilate any frame in a hurry.

Chapter 7

COME AS YOU ARE

ANOTHER evidence of gardening's adulthood and democracy is the clothes you wear for it. You may wear absolutely anything you please, or even nothing at all if you have nearsighted neighbors and no poison ivy on the place. If you stop to think of it, aren't other sports terribly snobbish about this? Take golf: after plus fours died (and until they did die, you were dead if you showed up on the links, as they quaintly called it then, in anything civilized), slacks came in. They are still in, along with Oxfords with fringe on top and blunt nails sticking out at the bottom. Gardeners who are having trouble aerating their bent grass have been known to entice these spike-shoed golfers into trotting all over their lawns by hinting there are lost golf balls to be found under the shrubs, like Easter eggs.

Officially there is no gardening costume. Of course, if anyone were so addled as to go poking into Abercrombie & Fitch, or Saks Fifth Avenue, asking about a gardening outfit, you could hardly expect them to chivvy him out.

Without a doubt he would be courteously measured
and clad, and told he was now equipped to grow a radish
fashionably. But even if he does then show up in tailored
denims and ten-dollar sunbonnets, he will find other
gardeners tolerant. Nobody will laugh. In fact, they won't
even notice what he is wearing. This alone has sent
thousands of prospective lady gardeners stomping off to
demand their money back and take up surfboard riding
instead.

Long before nice women were wearing slacks, let alone
Capri pants and skinny skintights—in the garden or out
of it—there was a neighbor woman where I lived as a
boy who gardened in her husband's trousers. He didn't
have many trousers, and I suppose she sometimes got
his best pair, because fierce fights between them would
break out, she in his pants in the back yard and he
bawling from their bedroom window. He was invariably
seedy from the waist down, though his coats were like
new.

Though there is no standard gardening outfit, it is not
a contradiction to say that by their clothes you may
know them. Therefore a ready reference to keep you up:

Tweed skirt, service-weight hose, sturdy Oxfords:
Here we have the non-nonsense British woman-gar-
dener type. She will doubtless be bearing an ancient
trowel in her right hand and in the left one a pot of
primroses perhaps, as if interrupted whilst stalking
across the moors. Her masculine counterpart may be

spotted by his Norfolk jacket with a bulge in one pocket. The bulge is an old leather pouch of shredded Virginia pipe tobacco.

Pretty girl in shorts and halter: Look harder—there's a boy next door, or in the immediate vicinity. The gardening here is strictly a prop.[1]

Picture hat, tea frock, flat basket for cut flowers over one arm: This one may throw you. Usually it is a dilettante. The veteran gardener carries a bucketful of water to plunge cut flowers in, and looks like the devil. But there is one exception—just as luncheon guests arrive, this same veteran may sometimes be seen stylishly sauntering about the garden, basket and all, as if there were no more to gardening than that.

Headful of curlers, robe or mussed dress: She'll be in a mad rush, too. This costume identifies the club woman. She really has no time to garden but works in a fast ten minutes after breakfast before breaking off to telephone a list of people about a bond issue. She gets something out of gardening, though, and it takes her gardener no more than an hour to put things back to rights.

Old clothes: Almost any kind of old clothes identify the genuine, or serious, gardener. It has often been remarked that a genuine gardener can turn new clothes into old clothes faster than anyone except an eight-year

[1] With one exception—brides. But they switch to blue jeans at about the same time the bridegroom skips his first weekend shave.

old boy on his way home from school. This applies to both men and women gardeners, neither of whom give a heck about how they look while gardening.[2]

The G.I. Look: Quickly spotted by the illusion you are passing a surprisingly residential-looking barracks, judging by the soldier boy in the yard. Actually he is an ex-soldier boy, wearing out his khaki uniforms. One of the best things you can say for khaki is that it's the color of mud.

I have heard rumors that the clothing manufacturers are thinking of trying zany fun clothes for male gardeners, on the order of those comic aprons for male barbecuers. If the clothing people want my advice, they may have it, free: Don't. Male gardeners would slash their wrists before they'd buy stuff like that. You'd go broke, fellows! (Confidentially, there are plenty of nuts who absolutely *would* buy such oddities, to amuse their gardening friends as gifts, but am I going to be such a fool as to breathe this to clothing manufacturers? Not if I am one of the gardening friends apt to be amused, and I fear the nuts outnumber us.)

[2] In fact, one wealthy male gardener I knew looked so disreputable in his garden clothes as he trimmed the front hedge, he was once asked by a passing minister new to the neighborhood why he didn't demand better wages for gardening so he could afford to dress more respectably. Rather than go into long explanations and possibly embarrass his wife, the man just said the job carried some good fringe benefits. "I get to sleep with the lady of the house, for one thing," he added, completely ending the chat.

Chapter 8

THE VISITING PLANT

EVERYTHING considered, I would rather have as a house guest my brother-in-law who sells encyclopedias," said a man of cool judgment and experience, "than any damned plant I know of." This gentleman's case was an aggravated one, perhaps, as he is married to a woman who can't say no to anybody who comes dragging along a potted plant to be tended while the owner is away. Also, she clusters such visiting plants in the bathroom for the sake of the humidity, and once kept a droopy *Monstera deliciosa* in the bathtub for two days, until her husband threatened to take a shower in the back yard in the buff under the lawn sprinkler. Nevertheless, the way he feels about the visiting plant is the way a lot of gardeners feel about it. Just because you garden doesn't mean you are fond of all plants.

Sometimes it seems as if going on a visit brings out the villainy in a plant. A begonia that has been happy as a tick in its swinging basket at home will start making as if to swoon the moment it realizes it has been fobbed off on the people next door to look after for two weeks. You'd suppose it would be grateful to them, but no, sir. Apparently all it can think of[1] is, who do its folks fancy they are, anyway, flipping off like this without it? And it determines to make them suffer.

The ones who suffer are the good Samaritans looking after it. In theory they could take a "suit yourself—live or die" attitude, but they don't. They worry. Only soft-hearted types who worry are ever asked to take on a guest plant. At its first show of wilting they rush to water it. They soak the daylights out of it in their anxiety and then have to punch holes in the potting mixture and try to dry it out before the roots all rot off. They could save their fretting, as none of this will make any difference, but by now they are blaming themselves and nothing is too good for the guest plant if it will p—l—e—a—s—e just last until its owners come home and reclaim it. So it gets quick-acting soluble fertilizer sprayed on its grumpy-looking leaves, and hourly changes of situation, to take advantage of sunlight and circulation, and fungicide just in case, and all-purpose bug spray to make sure. But this plant is determined to be miserable. Pretty soon its leaves begin falling off, hitting the floor with ominous swishes. Any blooms it may have will shatter. It begins to take on a decidedly undressed look, like a scrawny stripper toward the end of the act.

[1] Yes, think. Be patient and read on, please. This gets worse and worse.

This is seldom a fatal decline, though now and then a guest plant overdoes it and surprises itself by conking out. Nothing is so mortifying to the one who was supposed to be looking after the plant, but if the truth were known, quite a few of the owners are secretly relieved to come back and find a problem plant kaput and no fault of theirs. I know a woman in Pass Christian, Mississippi, who was so stunned to return from a glorious cruise and find her shrimp plant, left with neighbors, thriving, she happened to drop it on the way home. She dropped it on a stone sundial in the middle of a large, soft centipede-grass lawn, demolishing pot, plant, and all, and not doing the sundial any good either. It was a lamentable accident, she said, and skipped in to toss off a glass of sherry for comfort.

She should meet a man I know, fellow named Jack; lives in a Manhattan apartment. He is known among gardening friends as Jack the Nipper, because if you leave a plant with him to be looked after, sure as mortgages he nips it in the bud. He doesn't do this on purpose. He just naturally has a black thumb. The poor boy loves plants, too, but one and all they're allergic to him. Once somebody gave him a potted Jimson weed just to see what would happen. Lasted two days and then expired with a low rustle.

My wife, happening by just now, has remarked: "Don't forget the beast." It was our name for a plant we were saddled with for a couple of weeks by a friend who brought a list of instructions along with it (soil acidity

pH4, water daily, semishade . . .). "It eats flies, you
know," he said. "Three flies a day will do nicely." It was
one of the carnivorous plants; sticky, as I recall.

"Flies!" my wife said, leaning over for a closer look at
this monster. "Well, for heaven's sa . . ." She backed
off, reeling. The plant smelled like raw meat left in the
sun for days.

"That's how it attracts its prey," the owner said.
"After a while you get used to it. You don't even notice
it. Like ripe Camembert."

We had never been able to afford to get *that* used to
Camembert, and in the fortnight we had the carnivorous
plant neither of us grew blasé about it.

The season was a poor one for flies, and the plant
preferred them alive and struggling. At least it scorned
a plump one I swatted outside. "Too dead," my wife
said. "The instructions say 'living victims.'" I went outside again and presently returned with a bug in a bottle.
"What's that?" she asked.

"Bumble bee," I said, "and fighting mad. If it's sport
this plant wants . . ."

"Out!" she said, clutching her skirt about her knees.

"Well, unless it will consider worms," I said, "it's
going to be a mighty hungry flytrap two weeks from
today. We're out of bugs." She said we needed every
worm we had, and for several days she tempted the plant
with bits of steak, lowering them on a string to it as if
it were a shark. No good.

Then one day I twitched my nose. "Something smells
peculiar around here. Funny—I can't quite place—"

"It's fresh air," my wife said crisply. By George, she was right. "I banished that beast outside," she said, her back stiff. "I suppose it'll smell up the neighborhood, but I can't help that. I'm only human."

This desperate measure worked beautifully, to our amazement. Left on its own, the hungry plant put out so furious a stench, it lured bugs that had never bothered with us before. Even its owner remarked on its prosperous look when he came to get it (we whisked it back inside the house when we heard him coming), and seemed disappointed it had not missed him more.[2]

Well, to get back to that business about plants thinking. And feeling, too, though no gardener doubts they have feelings after he has once tried to please one determined to be pouty. When a plant has decided not to be pleased, you may as well go read a book or have a drink. Even that famous nurseryman's term, "tolerates so-and-so," won't do. A petulant plant will die before it stoops to tolerate.

As a matter of fact, a scientist who was fooling around with tomatoes a few years ago said that if a plant was thinking of dying, it was more susceptible to disease.[3] Makes them sound almost human, doesn't it?

[2] What we didn't know was that carnivorous plants also get nourishment the regular way from nutrients in the soil. They have about the highest standard of living in plant society.

[3] Dr. L. Ron Hubbard. He used a lie detector on the tomatoes. It registered their reaction to external influences, such as being jabbed with a nail. They hated it.

And researchers who were trying to grow plants upside down to get them ready for Lord knows what when we fly to the moon, found it didn't work because the plants got mad and quit. They didn't die; just stopped growing until working conditions improved.[4]

Air-minded people during the past few years have, in fact, been almost too much for plants to put up with, and the findings of the School of Aviation Medicine, Randolph Air Force Base, should be taken to heart by anybody who agrees to take care of a vacationing friend's plant. They found, these aviation medicine people, that irritated plants can and will poison the very air you breathe. They do it with the same stuff that comes out of your auto's exhaust, carbon monoxide. A mere two pounds of dried alfalfa leaves contain enough of this gas to kill a man if he is fool enough to breathe it in a confined space, such as a telephone booth.

While nobody is apt to ask you to look after an alfalfa plant for him, other plants can be just as mean about real or fancied slights. If you simply cannot avoid getting stuck with a visiting plant, maybe you'd better pay attention to what they're doing in Los Angeles. There, under the guidance of an organization called The Religious Research Foundation, Inc., people sing to plants— hymns, presumably—and radiate kind thoughts at them. They also say they are positive that plants do better in homes where everybody gets along beautifully.

[4] The researchers were working for the Republic Aviation Corporation. Researchers lead quietly turbulent lives.

Chapter 9

A ROSE LOVER IS A ROSE LOVER IS A ROSE LOVER

ONCE when I was working as a reporter on the St. Louis *Globe-Democrat,* the city editor sent me to interview the distinguished rosarian J. Horace McFarland, who was visiting the city. I knew nothing about roses except that they smelled nice, but things like that never bother city editors.[1] Dr. McFarland, a sprightly apple-cheeked man, saw right away that he would have to take me by the hand if he expected any decent position in the paper for the story, and he lost no time.

"Anybody who doesn't *love* roses should be prevented by law from growing them!" he declared in ringing

[1] Well, if we're going to be true-blue honest, some roses have hardly any fragrance—as will be noted a little farther along here —and one, the Austrian brier, smells bad though not everyone minds its rather animal odor. Its botanical name, *Rosa foetida,* means a rose that stinks.

tones. It made a headline the copy desk could throw its
heart into:

OUTLAW ROSE HATERS,
ROARS ROSY EXPERT

Dr. McFarland and I hit the front page, and it was
my initiation into rose-gardener psychology. Since then
I have known rose lovers who were so hipped on rose
loving that they suffered acutely when it was time to
prune the bushes. Or trees, as they like to call them for
some reason.

They refer to their pet as the queen of flowers, only
they capitalize it, and in their determination to be first
in everything they claim to have evidence through fossil
deposits that roses existed on earth thirty-five or even
seventy million years ago, so had to wait a good spell
before there were any human rose lovers around to love
them.

They also quote extensively from literature to show
how poets appreciated roses. Shakespeare, Omar Khay-
yam, and Sappho are among those mentioned. Banquet
halls in ancient times, they add casually, were strewn
with rose petals, and so were beds, making everything
pretty skiddy. And there was the War of the Roses, too,
and to hear rosarians talk, you'd almost think the roses
were the most important things *in* the war.[2] And then,

[2] A variety (versicolor) of the damask rose is the York and
Lancaster rose of the War of Roses fame. White and pink ones
are often found on the same bush; also pink-and-white-striped
ones. Botanical name: *Rosa damascena.* A very old species.

more than three centuries later, Napoleon's Josephine attracted all kinds of attention by scouring the world by proxy for roses galore to grow in the palace gardens at Malmaison. Rose lovers never let you forget such titbits. Small wonder some gardeners think the biggest obstacle to loving roses is rose lovers.

Like all specialists, rose gardeners are loaded with just-so techniques on the culture of their darlings. Some of the cultural instructions are couched in pretty poignant prose. Speaking of picking a site for the rose bed, for example, one authority said: "Roses must smile at the sun, moon, and stars." No rose lover would think there was anything unusual about this phrasing. Some rosarians think roses must have their feet, as they put it, in clay to do well. My wife and I once lived next door to a man who paid dearly to have a ton or two of sticky yellow clay hauled about fifty miles, to replace the black, humus-rich topsoil of the countryside in the spot roses were to go. I must admit the roses grew about as well in the clay as they did in the topsoil for others in the neighborhood.

All rose growers seem devoted to manure for the rose garden. Reminds me of something else Dr. McFarland said during that interview. "Even if he has to steal it," he said, "a rose lover is entitled to manure for his roses." He added that it wasn't really stealing, and I suppose he meant it was horticultural socialism.

There used to be an elderly woman in the country around Chevy Chase, Maryland, who constantly carried a shovel and bucket in her car to gather any manure she came across on rural roads. Everybody except rose lovers thought her eccentric. They merely admired her bravery in the teeth of the traffic, which she declined to yield to while shoveling. She survived the traffic, to die eventually of indignation brought on by the growing scarcity of horses.

Some rose lovers pretend to believe that everybody is fond of roses—all roses. When speaking of choosing varieties, one said jauntily: "Anyone has likes and dislikes —that is, if anyone can be found who dislikes a rose." Listen, not only are there persons who dislike a rose, there are those who dislike all roses. There are even rose fanciers who scorn whole entire species of roses. One who comes to mind is a retired scientist who likes only old species. His southern rose garden is made up of the old tea roses, with a scattering of cabbage roses, China roses, hybrid perpetuals, and so on. Friends have innocently enraged him now and then by bringing him hybrid tea rose bushes, imagining that he loved roses in general. Ho! There is, it happens, one hybrid tea in his entire garden grounds—a white La France, which squeaked by on its historical interest, since La France was the first hybrid tea rose in the world, developed in 1876. He keeps it in a pot, where it can be quickly shoved behind the greenhouse door when visitors drop by.[3]

[3] The original La France is pink, actually. The white is a mutation of this. Ask the average nurseryman for La France today, and he'll wonder if you also wear congress boots and carry a snuffbox.

Tea roses, by the way, were so named because it was thought they smelled like tea. (Some think the namer must have meant the tea plant flower.) The same reasoning brought about the naming of the musk rose, which to some smells of musk, which is the same as saying a whiff of skunk. The Bourbon rose does not smell of bourbon, though, and neither does the cabbage rose follow this party line. The Bourbon, a cross of the Provence and China roses, was developed on the Isle of Bourbon, and the "cabbage" in the other name refers to the wealth of petals. You'd think they could have found a better comparison, wouldn't you? Almost anything would have been better. Speaking of fragrances, the damask rose smells so fine, it is used for attar of roses. So is *Rosa alba*, another species not much seen these days.

If you aren't sick and tired of hearing about rose smells, we may as well finish it off by mentioning that over fifty different odors have been cited to try and pin down how various roses smell—like oranges, peaches, honey, nuts, grapes, spices, and so on—all of which shows how right Alexander Graham Bell was when he told a graduating class years ago to try measuring a smell if they wanted a challenging research job. And in case you think modern roses don't smell as good as old ones, a team of scientists in 1950 smelled six hundred important species, old and new, and found no differences based on species age. They did find, to the chagrin of the rose lovers among them, that a whopping third of all roses haven't enough fragrance to talk about. Another third are merely moderately fragrant, leaving it up to the last third to keep everybody thinking all roses smell just wonderful.

If a Hollywood actress had a fan club as active and loyal as the fan club the rose has, no studio could afford her. The name of the rose's fan club is the American Rose Society, with more than sixteen thousand members in I don't know how many cities and hamlets, 350 or more affiliated clubs, and lobbyists in Washington trying to get the rose voted our national flower.[4] Not satisfied with politicking, the society is also out to make everybody love roses. "A Rose for Every Home, a Bush for Every Garden," is the way their ambitious motto reads, in a ragtime swing reminiscent of "A chicken in every pot, a car in every garage." That one didn't make the grade in its time either.

One of the things the society does is to score the roses, as if they were students. An absolutely perfect rose would get ten points, and anything below six points is failing, though a low-score rose may have some very good characteristics. No rose has yet scored ten points, but the society keeps hoping. And each year another organization, All-America Rose Selections, tests new roses on twenty-

[4] This infuriates people who have commercial interests in, or great fondness for, other flowers. Each time the well-organized rose people show up in the capital, they are eyed evilly by advocates of other contenders for national flower—the marigold, corn tassel, carnation, columbine ... the list seems endless and includes even grass. So far, nobody has had the nerve to suggest a national vegetable.

two trial grounds to find the best ones. It is things like this that make the rose fanciers seem so snobbish to other gardeners.

If it will help cheer up these non-rose lovers—rose gardeners have more than their share of pests. Starting with ants and aphis, the list of merely the ordinary pests runs to twenty or so, and there are also nine or ten diseases as common as measles and chicken pox among children.[5]

On the other side of the coin, roses have been touted as cure-alls for many things that trouble humans. These include loose teeth, watering eyes, and hang-overs. Speaking of hang-overs, the Persians made a strong wine of rose petals, and soon after the Norman invasion of England a rose-petal liqueur was being made there. Today in England they make jam out of rose petals. There's a comedown for you. This does not mean that the rose is regarded less fondly in England than it was, though. It is the English national flower, and they are so serious about it that when the roses in Kew Gardens began looking tired recently, questions were raised about them in the House of Lords. Turned out that a gardener with his mind on fish and chips very likely had sprayed the

[5] One rose gardener who found himself finally too short of time and energy for the everlasting spraying and dusting simply stopped. Reminded me of an aunt of mine who said she couldn't afford the income tax. The rose man has got on surprisingly well without spraying or dusting, and my aunt never did go to jail.

roses with weed killer. In Henry VIII's time he'd have lost his moony head.

Ancient Romans used to swear by powdered roses for relieving the bite of a sea dragon. Had they eaten the rose hips instead, they would have got a rousing good dose of Vitamin C, and it might have helped them resist the barbarians. At any rate, it would have helped them resist scurvy.

Chapter 10

ORGANIC—ER—GARDENING

S OME people say: "Shoot an organic gardener, and you'll kill a nut." In an effort to determine the true pro and con of organic gardening today, I decided to take a poll . . .[1]

---

[1] It convinced me. Convinced me *I'd* be a nut to get mixed up in this rhubarb. In the interval since my wife and I did our stint at amateur organic gardening of sorts, tempers have frayed, challenges have roared. What with the urban sprawl, pesticides, bureaucracy, and the new leisure, things are in an even worse state than usual between organic zealots and the rest of the world. If I sound as cautious as the fellow who wrote people insulting letters in invisible ink and then didn't mail them, that'll just have to be the way it goes.

Chapter 11

GARDEN TOURS AND DETOURS

T HE secret of a successful garden tour is timing,"
one authority has stated. I can add another secret.
It is: The secret of a successful garden tour is to
deal only with lady gardeners.

Not that male gardeners won't agree to an organized
tour of their gardens. Some will once. Twice, almost
never. They may not refuse outright, but they will dream
up trips out of town, seizures of melancholia, measles—
anything to duck the honor. My wife and I have a bachelor gardening friend who was even sneakier about it. His
garden is one of those show places, with broad grassed
avenues clipped close, nothing but peatmoss for mulch,
all faded blossoms and fallen leaves gathered each morning, metal labels on everything, and so forth. Came the
day he was asked to be included on the local garden
club's spring garden tour, and not feeling himself that
day, he agreed.

He was expecting, for some odd reason, a small study
group of earnest women gardeners with notebooks and

horn-rimmed glasses. That's bachelors for you. What he got was a thundering invasion of happy gossip and chiffon that swept over him and his garden like the Japanese beetle plague. The year following this Donnybrook, when the advance scout for the ladies came waltzing back, he was ready for her. Oh, be delighted to have the garden tour again, he said through clenched teeth, *providing* a few rules were observed. He had written them down so there would be no trouble understanding them:

1. No high heels. Stocking feet preferred.
2. No cigarettes, candy, chewing gum allowed.
3. No fool questions.
4. No touching anything.
5. Absolutely no straying from paths.
6. No flimsy clothes that thorns can tear.
7. Positively adults only!
8. Tour limited to five minutes per head and no repeats.
9. Leave loose clutter such as handbags in cars.
10. Before starting tour, everyone will kindly sign release form to be provided, holding owner harmless in case of injury, agreeing to abide by above rules, and agreeing not to break off canes, branches, etc., for slips or any other purpose.

He considered including an eleventh point providing for frisking any suspiciously bulky dame on leaving, but decided it might be misunderstood. He didn't have to bother with it anyway, because when the tour representative got her breath back, she said it was awfully

sweet of him, she was sure, and they'd discuss it and let
him know. Apparently they've been discussing it for the
seven years since then, as he gets quite a few snippy looks
in public and hasn't seen hide nor hair of the girls at
his garden gate again.

If he had been a husband instead of a bachelor, things
would have been different. A woman loves to show off
her garden to other women, although you'd never know
it to see her looking the garden over right after she's
been asked. What seemed a pretty jazzy patch of posies
before suddenly looks to her like a vacant lot the kids
have been playing cops and robbers in. Leaves that were
green an hour ago are now yellow, the edges of borders
are as ragged as a home haircut, buds have balled, die-
back has set in, and a sickly pallor hangs in the air. Or
so it seems to the poor wretch. At this point women have
been known to go frantic, dash for the telephone, and
order vast potted-plant replacements from the nursery
for immediate delivery, plus four men at time-and-a-half
to put them in. Nurserymen who have gone into the
nursery business because they were seeking peace and
quiet sometimes wonder if it is all a bad dream.

Incidentally, this is one place where it takes a gardener
to understand a gardener. There was the case of the
three ladies in Webster Groves, Missouri. Two were
dedicated gardeners and also next-door neighbors. The
third played bridge and things. One summer a civic club
they all belonged to decided to raise funds with a garden
tour instead of its usual rummage sale. The two garden-

ing ladies worked themselves to tatters, edging and pruning and timing blooms and making sure colors in adjoining borders didn't clash, and all that kind of meti-
culous detailing. The tour was a big success, and in a
couple of months the two gardening ladies' hands were
almost cleaned up and smoothed enough so that they
could face a manicurist again at last. That was when the
non-gardening, bridge-playing lady happened to speak
up over a cup of tea, and said to them: "I think we
ought to have another garden tour next year—it's more
fun than a rummage sale and *so* much less work."

Small wonder, too, that the husband of a woman
gardener who is getting ready to hostess a tour would
rather go through two house cleanings. It isn't just the
turmoil of her getting things ready and the cold cuts he
gets for dinner that prey on his mind. There is also his
wife's twitchings and shudders as she cranks up to
the big day and, when it arrives, pins on a brilliant
smile, prays that the tour's publicity chairman will have
pull enough to whistle up a newspaper photographer
while she still looks human, and keeps one ear permanently tuned to catch what visitors say about her efforts
as they troop through. Only after it is all over and the
last visitor has left can the wife turn her mind again to
practical matters and nurse her husband back to sanity.

Chapter 12

"DID YOU EVER TASTE ANYTHING SO GOOD IN YOUR LIFE?"

SOME vegetable gardeners deny they grow the most delectable stuff they ever ate, and they probably lie about other things, too. On the other hand, you can trust a gardener who yanks a radish out of the ground, wipes it on his pants, and hands it to you to enjoy on the spot. You'd better eat it. One of these days you may want to put the grip on him for an armload of roasting ears, to go with steaks on the patio.

The chances are, he'll not only supply the ears, if he likes you, but he'll organize things to make sure they're cooked right. And by "right" he'll mean as soon after picking as is humanly possible.[1] A roasting-ears admirer will synchronize his watch with that of the cook, time his arrival in the corn patch to coincide with the barbe-

[1] He has a point. Sweet corn's sugar starts changing to starch within seconds after the ear is pulled from the stalk. You can slow it down by keeping the ears in the refrigerator, but don't serve them much later to a sweet-corn gourmet.

cue grill's period of temperature perfection, and then race with the pulled ears the moment he's pulled them. This is ridiculous, of course, unless you love corn on the cob, and if you don't, you must be a communist.

Furthermore you ought to be thankful he *wants* to cook the corn. Or maybe you haven't run into the "they're-so-good-we-always-eat-'em-raw" gardener? He not only eats 'em raw—he doesn't even wait to get them to the table. Chomping your way through his garden with him is an experience in sampling lima beans on the half shell, broccoli sprouts ("Go ahead and try them—they aren't sprayed"; you know it's true, the cabbage worms look so healthy), young beets and turnips (not as bad as they sound, if washed first), okra pods (can't recommend them), squash and green tomatoes (no, thanks).

However, even cooked, and well cooked, vegetables can miss the target. Depends on who's eating them. I knew a career girl who happened to be a vegetable gardener, and one day she decided she wasn't getting any younger and she'd better start fascinating an eligible outdoorsy sort of man she'd been dating and who looked at times as if he had the makings of a husband. She asked him over to her house for dinner, and since the garden was outdoing itself just then with lush production, she had a wonderful selection of things.

Her menu ran like this: Leek-and-celery soup; lettuce-and-endive salad; parsnip fritters; and Italian zucchini squash casserole with plenty of sweet basil and parsley; and something she called tomato triumph. She served carrot pudding for dessert and found time to remark once or twice that everything but the butter, salt, and pepper had come right out of the garden. By mid-meal her boy friend was swallowing with difficulty and seemed to have trouble thinking of anything to say.

When he left, which he did right after the pudding, he was walking like a man someone had been dropping watermelons on, and she made a mental note to see if he needed new glasses. But after several days had passed with not a peep out of him, she became concerned and made inquiries. "Gone off on a long hunting trip," one of his friends told her. "Yep, said he figured it'd take him the first two weeks just to make up lost ground, whatever that means."

Chapter 13

"HERE KITTY, KITTY, KITTY, KITTY!"

IF GARDENERS were gardeners and pet lovers were pet lovers, things would be a lot simpler. There was an engineer, lived and worked in Ohio, who retired without any of the qualms retirement sometimes brings, because he knew exactly what he was going to do. He was going to have time to fool around with irises to his heart's content. He hybridized irises, and it was a full and satisfying hobby. So far, so good. Then some well-meaning bumbler gave him a puppy. It would be company for him now that he was retired, the donor said.

Company was right. It was so much company for him that he hardly had time to say a kind word to his irises while he saw the pup through worming, teething, housebreaking, and slipper-worrying. But when the pup grew up, you say, he surely had leisure to resume his iris interest? Yes, he did. Trouble was, this pup had a St. Bernard for a father and something about the size of a haystack for a mother, evidently. When he was six months old, he weighed more than the engineer, and every time he galloped through an iris bed—zong. It is possible the man could have solved the problem by giving the vast beast away, had he known any dog-loving dwellers on the Great Plains. By this time, though, he had grown quite dotty about it, and philosophical about the irises. "Quadrant really doesn't do much damage," he would murmur, gathering up shattered stems and blossoms, and scandalized rhizomes. "And besides, you know, some interesting polyploid effects sometimes result from trauma." [1]

Trauma does have its supporters, as witness a letter from a woman gardener whose husband had long wanted a Norwegian elkhound. Finally he got the elkhound, and it turned out to be quite a handful. "Ralph has just gone out again to raise all the fences by still another foot," wrote this lady, "though I have come to believe that nothing on earth can keep Buster permanently inside the yard. However, having a forty-pound dog dashing all over the grounds has greatly simplified my life. There is hardly a shrub or a flower border worth bothering my head about any more, and at last I have the time to take up piano, painting, square dancing, breadmaking, and golf."

A related situation came about when a cagey fellow who owned a dachshund moved into a duplex owned by

[1] Scar tissue may result in new cells with more than the normal complement of heredity carriers—chromosomes. Among other things, this can bring new colors in flowers, and irises in particular have greatly benefited through polyploidy, as such an increase is called. The chances are, though, all you'll get from beating your plants is a lot of mad plants.

a single woman. She said he could keep the dog if it got along with her cat, but it positively had to stay out of the yard, which was crammed with flowers. He agreed, and took the dog out for six or eight walks a day, until they were both so full of fresh air they were bow-legged. Then one day the man sauntered in with a handful of curly black fur. "What's that?" his landlady exclaimed.

"Pup," he said. "Friend of mine it belongs to can't keep it but hasn't the heart to have it put to sleep." He held the pup up, and it ran its little red tongue out and wagged its stub tail at the woman. "Don't worry—I'm not going to keep it either," the man said. "On my way to the Humane Society with it." He paused. "They gas 'em," he said. "S—s—s—s—t! No more pup." The landlady batted her eyes. "Before I go, though, I have to phone somebody about something," he said, "and I'd be obliged if you'd keep an eye on the pup." He handed it over, went into his own quarters and had a good cigar and a glass or two of Duff Gordon dry.

"All set," he said, appearing at the landlady's door again. She and the pup weren't there. Nobody there but the cat, looking sore. He traced the landlady and the pup to the garden. The pup was racing through the petunias, mashing down the lobelia, ripping out the portulaca. The landlady was sitting on the grass, clapping her hands.

"Don't you lay a finger on this pup, you murderer, you," she said calmly. "It's mine now."

He coughed politely, gazed at the sky and then at the pup, now sitting on a begonia. "Ah . . ." the landlady murmured, "wouldn't your little dachshund like to play with him . . . here?" And that was that.

You may have noticed that the cat in this story wasn't mentioned as having any interest in gardening. Actually, a number of gardeners are cat owners, and many have good words to say for cats as garden companions. An exception was a charming little woman we'll call Mary, since that's her name, who got herself a garden cat in order to keep down the gophers that were driving her wild. She called the cat Isis, after the Egyptian goddess, and this was a mistake. The cat began to put on airs, and pretty soon decided that hunting gophers was beneath her. This made Mary so indignant she stopped calling the cat Isis and switched to Kitty. Too late. By now the cat was hopelessly in love with the image it was projecting, and Mary's roaring: "Here Kitty, Kitty, Kitty, Kitty!" was futile. All it got her was a raw throat and an offer from the neighbors to lend her a gopher trap free.

I meant to say that some dogs are themselves gardeners if given a chance. One woman was entertaining a friend's Yorkshire terrier one spring, and she let him come into the garden because he seemed too little to do any harm. In fact, his name was Eenie-Weenie, and he weighed two pounds less than the telephone directory. He was thrilled to come into the garden and showed an intelligent interest in the seeds she was working with. Some days later the woman was baffled to find something like 150 squash plants sprouting in one little spot the size of a cookie, about 300 mustard plants in another tiny place, and 500 lettuce plants in a third. She did some probing with a trowel and found, sure enough, a beautifully planted seed packet in each spot.

She had already fired off a tart letter to the seed house she dealt with, and now for a few moments she wrestled with her conscience about following up the letter with an apology from the dog and her. In the end she decided this would probably confuse things even more, so she just let them send her the replacement packets of squash, mustard, and lettuce she had demanded, and sent them a thank-you note when they arrived under cover of a form apology that told her mistakes did sometimes happen in filling orders, and they hoped she would forgive them.

A male gardener who liked company while in his garden but didn't want to take on a dog decided to try a myna bird. The myna was quite a talker, and the two of them rattled away for a few weeks, though the myna was handicapped by having to answer every remark with such general replies as "How are you?" The partnership broke up finally when the bird took to whistling at passing girls and gave the gardener an interesting reputation in the neighborhood.

And then there was Kathleen, an artist who had a pet rattlesnake in her Arizona desert garden. It wasn't a pet at first, but Kathleen said she sang to it and this gentled it. She wouldn't say what she sang, but this went on for months, until a shocked neighbor happened to almost step on the sing-happy rattler as it tangoed across the artist's driveway.

He promptly atomized it with a charge of buckshot, breathing hard. The immediate result was the overrunning of the place with all kinds of rattlesnakes—big, little, and middle-class. All mean, too; not a music lover among them. "It's plain to see my nice big snake had been keeping all those bad ones away," Kathleen later said sadly. "Sure, and you'd think some people could mind their own business, now, wouldn't you?"

Chapter 14

HOW TO MAKE A GARDENER
DELIRIOUSLY HAPPY, OR
AT LEAST DELIRIOUS

A BLUNT man I know, named Lyon, has a succinct piece of advice he is willing to give anybody: "If you are introduced to somebody and find out he is a gardener, drop the acquaintance at once." The reason for this dictum, which he calls Lyon's Law, is that if you continue the acquaintance, you will eventually find yourself knee-deep in spare plants, cuttings, bulbs, seeds, rhizomes, clumps, and roots. Being a veteran gardener himself, he knows what he is talking about. If he were a dewy new gardener, he would be deliriously happy to get the free offerings, but he ran out of garden space and spare time ten years ago.

It is a rare gardener who can throw away the surplus plant material that gradually accumulates as he prunes and thins and divides. He may even be sentimental about it. He gives it to his friends, to acquaintances, to strangers

66

—even to enemies if they'll promise not to bring it back. Some gardeners have been pushed to skulking around after dark and leaving their surplus stuff on doorsteps, nearly scaring the pajamas off the male neighbors when they step out for the newspaper next morning and find tidy little bundles of something waiting for them.

A wholesale solution for the problem is used in one community—Monterey, California. Here the city holds an annual Cutting Day, and those who have surplus cuttings or anything else bring them, and those who want the stuff come and get it, free. Trouble is, gardeners who arrive loaded down with things they are thankful to get rid of are sometimes so tempted by things other over-burdened gardeners have dumped there that they leave with more than they brought. Somebody should organize a Gardeners Anonymous for people such as these.

We once lived on the same street as a man who was planting a vegetable garden for the first time in his life. It seemed to be mainly in sweet corn, and he got wonderful germination, so that presently he realized he'd have to thin; he had planted the seeds practically side by side. But when he started pulling sprouts out, he didn't have the heart to throw them away. He went up and down the street with a boxful of the seedlings, trying to find homes for them as if they were kittens.

People told him you couldn't transplant corn, but you know how beginners are. He brought his seedlings home again and transplanted as many as he could, in a place his wife had planned for chrysanthemums. A few grew to maturity and gave him a late crop of ears, and when experienced gardeners told him he could get the same thing the next year with a tenth the trouble by seeding a late crop, he said never mind, gardening was too anguishing for a tender heart, and he was giving it up.

Unfortunately, gardeners aren't the only ones who burden gardeners with misguided gifts for the garden. We come now to two sad cases. One involved a couple who had a nice weekend place in Mississippi on a bayou. One of their joys was a lavish growth of wild azaleas on a woodsy patch of the grounds, on the slope down to the bayou. They were generous with their place and often let friends use it, though the owners didn't expect them to work on it or anything. Well, one such party of friends decided to show their gratitude just the same, by tidying things up outside, and I suppose you can guess what happened.

"They tidied the living hell out of it," the owner said later. "Rooted out every one of our wild azaleas. Said they thought they'd save us the trouble of clearing underbrush in the woods. What did we do? What *could* we do? We had to grit our teeth and *thank* them!"

The other case is curiously opposite. The victims here were a couple who had retired to a splendidly placed home on the California coast, where they could sit on the patio of an evening sipping daiquiris and watching the sun go down in the Pacific Ocean. It was something

they had talked of doing for years. Now they were happy
doing it.

Then they went to Europe for three months, and a
rich uncle stayed in their house for the interval. They
refused rent, so he decided to do something handsome
for them, and he hit on the idea of planting the grounds.
This was virgin territory, as the couple had merely an easy
bit of lawn and a few understanding geraniums.

Not one to do things by halves, Uncle yelled for a
landscape architect, who rapidly sketched out something
along the lines of the Hanging Gardens of Babylon and
sent a wave of prosperity through the local nurseries.
When the couple returned, every inch of their grounds
was planted with lusty shrubs, blooming blooms, hedges,
and even full-grown trees. The lawn had been dug up
and replaced with a more aristocratic turf; there were
paths of smooth white pebbles; a hundred roses bloomed
around a brand-new lily pool with fountain. Hydrangeas
bordered one wall of the house, azaleas, rhododendrons,
and fuchsias the others. There were lime and lemon
trees already bearing, and baskets of ferns and begonias
dangled from the roof overhang. The couple was almost
overcome, you can imagine. They said it was the most
wonderful thing that had ever happened to anybody, and
Uncle said tut, tut, the pleasure was all his.

He was right, too. No more sprawling around watching sunsets for those two. Can't keep your mind on a
sunset when the weeds are taking over the roses, and the
fuchsias are fainting, and grass is springing up in the

paths and dying on the lawn. With all these improvements, every day brought its emergency. The couple
bought an alarm clock and began to get up an hour
earlier for fast pruning and edging before breakfast. They
turned down evening engagements to keep from yawn-
ing in people's faces, and dropped their golf club mem-
bership.

After three months of this, the husband stopped being
retired and took a job. He used the salary to hire a full-
time gardener. On weekends and after he got home from
work each day, the husband found he could do some of
the things his wife and the gardener were too rushed to
get at, and in this way they have kept from falling more
than a day or two behind each week. Uncle visits them
occasionally, but not as often as before. He says privately
that they're not as much fun as they used to be. Must be
getting old or something.

Chapter 15

WATERING, WATERING, EVERYWHERE

THERE was once a gardener who grew so bored with the shrill demands of his garden for water—help!—water—that he made up his mind to raise absolutely nothing but cacti. The poor fellow had squandered five or six hundred dollars on cacti galore before he found out that they, too, need water. Only difference is, they don't blow it all in the minute they get it.[1]

Watering is one of the least understood of gardening needs. (Some of the others are sunlight, drainage, soil handling, seeding, fertilizing, cultivating, mulching, pest control, and frost protection.) If you could actually see water being used by plants it would help explain all sorts of things. For instance—

[1] Oh, well, it's not quite that bad. Most of the one-thousand-plus species of the cactus family (*Cactaceae*) take a winter rest of six to eight months. Need no water to speak of during this time, including house-plant cacti. But when they aren't resting, they appreciate water as much as any of us. They *can* get along with very little then, but won't do much growing or any blooming.

(Note: It is suggested that gardeners who are feeling tired lie down during the next paragraph, or skip it entirely until they are stronger.)

Now, then—for instance: The average plant will evaporate through its leaves in a single season water equal to four hundred times the plant's dry weight at season's end. To match this, a person would have to guzzle about twenty pints each and every day. The next time you see a fifty-pound bale of hay, reflect that it took twenty thousand pints of water to grow it. With facts like this at your fingertips you can be the life of a party.

Trees are also great for water. A tree thinks nothing of tossing off fifty gallons a day. One tree can keep a small spring busy. And in case you wonder why some parts of your lawn, garden, or borders seem to need more water than others, trees may be the reason. The average tree acts as if it expects a drought any minute and is worried to death. It sponges up water so fast that little brother grass or anything else is lucky to get a sip if the tree's mattress of roots is underneath. A tree's roots are supposed to extend about as far from its trunk as its branches do, but trees have their own notions about this and may send roots off limits.

One of the classic foolers that haunt new gardeners is the rule: When you water, water thoroughly. If "thoroughly" means to get water to the deepest roots—well, some plants are happy with roots no longer than your finger, and others burrow restlessly down six and eight feet and more. To make it still more confusing, wet weather when a crop is getting started can be a drawback; it coddles the plants, and they may not bother to grow good long roots. Then they get caught in dry spells later, like children who never had to earn any money until they grew up.

If you're a glutton for figures, here are a few on soil absorption: Say you put an inch and a half of water down with a sprinkler. (You can measure by setting a few tin cans around to catch the spray.) The inch and a half of water will moisten a clay soil nine inches deep, and a sandy soil just twice as deep—eighteen inches. A loam soil will be in the middle—moist for twelve inches down.

As long as we are on distances, we may as well taper off on water here with a word on spacing. When a seedsman tells you to space tomato plants two feet apart, one of the things he is basing it on is the average rainfall. The "average" in average rainfall is about as capricious as the average average woman, but you can't blame the seedsman for that. So, if the season is dry his spacing will be too close, and how do you tell when plants are suffering from thirst?

Most of us go by the wilting rule: A plant will tell you it needs water, by wilting. This is a yes-and-no thing. Some plants are so independent, they refuse to wilt (until it's too late to do much for them, that is; they wilt eventually). Some of these, instead of wilting, simply stop growing. Others get so worked up, they go dormant. A thirsty tomato turns its lower leaves a deeper green, and so do cucumbers. Corn leaves curl, some other plants become permanent runts, and so it goes.

Some experienced gardeners stick a finger into the soil to test for moisture, and it seems to work pretty well for them. If you live near such a gardener, one way is to water whenever he does. Then, if anything goes wrong, you've got somebody to blame.

And speaking of that, there was an engineer whose wife was a gardener, and he was a great help to her, though he was no more interested in gardening than in cutting out paper dolls. The thing was, she was almost 100 per cent unmechanical-minded; even had to concentrate hard when she drove a wheelbarrow. So that's where he came in. Well, one year he decided that the watering chore was too hard on her, and he worked out and installed a big sprinkler system with a grid of underground pipes covering their grounds, and with forty sprinkler heads, spaced every few feet. He put in a booster pump to get pressure to run the system, and this was an impressive thing when finished. From a central control point you turned one valve for the left front yard, another for the right front yard, another for the rear left quadrant, etc. Worked like a dream except for one item: his wife couldn't get the hang of all those valves.

When the engineer caught her watering with a sprinkling can, he went to work again on the problem, and this time came up with an automatic timer that turned the water on and off without the help of human hands. He was going to add some other improvements, such as a switch-in tank of soluble fertilizer on the line, but postponed further work while he went off to attend an engineers' convention. When he came back, two weeks later, he asked his wife how the automatic sprinkling system had been working.

Just like clockwork, she said. Every sprinkler on the place had turned on every afternoon right on schedule and had watered vigorously for two hours. There was, in fact, only one thing that needed some tinkering with. What was that? asked the engineer, making for his tool box.

It was the weather, his wife said. While he had been gone, it had rained almost constantly, and every day at four o'clock, as the forty sprinklers whooshed their spray up into the downpour, she had had to spend all her time on the telephone explaining to people that she really was feeling quite normal, thanks, and that unless they also were married to an engineer it was impossible for them to understand her situation.

Chapter 16

THE WEATHER BE DAMNED

SPEAKING of the weather as villain, I was on the point of saying that house-plant gardeners and greenhouse gardeners are the only ones who can laugh at the weatherman, but then I remembered the Kuypers, and that knocked off the house-plant crowd. The Kuypers were in their sixties when my wife and I knew them, and they had started a house-plant collection in their thirties. Mr. Kuyper could take house plants—and any other plants—or leave them alone, but his wife regarded each one as a personality. Consequently, she wanted to see them happy, and if you were a plant would you be happy stuck inside the house during the nice weather?

So each spring, on a balmy Saturday morning, Mr. Kuyper did his setting-up exercises for the season by carrying all the plants outdoors. While they had been growing bigger and older, he had merely been growing older, until with some that had developed into trees, practically, he could hardly make it. And each fall, of course, he had to do it all over again in reverse before first frost.

Scientists will tell you that one of these days man will control the weather, but not many gardeners believe this. The nearest thing to it was the conviction of an elderly woman gardener that all it took to make the weather behave itself was prayer. Then one season an untimely spring drought killed off her entire balsam border while she was away visiting the grandchildren, and she was so put out when she came back that she changed churches.

The same viewpoint was held by the old lady who was miffed by being accidentally omitted from her minister's garden party invitations, and who told him, when he apologetically asked her at the last minute: "It's too late. I've already prayed for rain."

The weather—or climate, to use the broader term—is one of the Big Three that affect the growth of plants, and in fact determine whether the dratted things will grow at all. The other two factors are soil properties, and man along with other animals and plants. You can sum it up by adding that moisture, sunshine, and temperature account for most of the weather.

If gardeners behaved like gardens, they would sit around dozing all winter, and the garden-supply ad writers would go mad. But until the weather warms up, plants just aren't interested. And then, like people, they get annoyed if it warms up too much. For one thing, hot weather competes with the plant for soil moisture. As a result, some realistic plants do best in cool climates and are willing to endure being chilly to avoid being thirsty. Most plants, however, expect pie in the sky and make trouble if they don't get it.

Every gardener knows that most plants want plenty of sunshine, but if you could speak to a plant about it, you might be surprised. "Sunshine, yes—but not such sunny sunshine," is what you'd hear from most of them.[1]

The fact is, the length of the day means a lot more to a plant than how bright the sun is. Plants knew all about daylight saving long before man even knew about clocks. If a plant wants long days, nothing else will do, and the same goes for short-day plants. Some plants don't mind what length the day is, and are considered rather common by the others.

Every plant resents being moved from the climate it likes best, and shows it by making all sorts of demands if you expect it to stay alive in strange territory. This is no news to most gardeners, of course, but it hardly ever keeps them from trying their luck with unacclimated things. I knew a Missouri gardener who felt it an outrage that nature didn't consider Missouri proper country for growing globe artichokes. He was passionately fond of the

[1] For instance, the light intensity at noon on a bright summer day in the Midwest can amount to ten-thousand foot-candles. A plant can thrive on a few hundred foot-candles. The sunlight an American plant wastes in a day would feed a European plant for weeks.

things and often complained that he couldn't even find where to buy the plants, roots, or whatever you used, to try and grow his own.

Then one day he got his hands on a catalog that listed artichokes, and he fired off an order. In due time a package of tubers arrived, and he planted them in the nicest place in the garden, yelling back over his shoulder to his wife to start practicing up on hollandaise sauce.

Having never even seen artichokes growing, he was not surprised when his plants went gawking up until they were taller than he, though a good deal skinnier, something like sunflowers. This went on for some while, and no sign of anything that looked like any artichoke *he* had ever seen. He became more and more restive, and finally in early fall his wife had an inspiration. "Do you suppose," she asked, "that perhaps they grow underground?"

Pretty grim by now, the man yanked one of the plants out of the ground. On its roots were a lot of tubers like the ones he had planted, looking like lumpy weenies, not a bit like globe artichokes. He wrapped one up and sent it off with a hot letter to the catalog house that had sold him the things, and back came a cool answer:

DEAR SIR:

This *is* an artichoke—not a globe artichoke but a Jerusalem artichoke, as plainly stated in our catalog, as you can see by rereading the listing. We are sorry you misunderstood, but suggest you try this vegetable, a delicacy in its own right.

He was so upset, he wouldn't have anything to do with his crop of Jerusalem artichokes, a couple of bushels. His wife hated to waste anything, so she ate them, trying out all the recipes the catalog people had kindly sent along with their letter. Unfortunately, by the time she finished off the second bushel, she had formed a craving for the damned things, and her husband had to include them in his garden from then on.

Chapter 17

CACTUS ON THE FIRE ESCAPE

A CAREER girl who was lying late abed in her
New York brownstone apartment one Sunday
morning suddenly thought she saw a vine growing down from the headboard of her bed. Since this was
plainly nonsense, she went back to sleep, and when she
awoke again later, the vine had grown six or eight inches
and was making for her throat. This got her out of bed,
you can bet, and she snatched up the first weapon that
came to hand—a satin mule—and beat the vine savagely
until it was limp. Then she got a steak knife, traced the
defeated vine to a crack in the wall behind her bed, and
cut it off.

At this point, breathing hard, she began to wonder
how the vine had got there, and what would have happened if she had not awakened in time, so she dressed
and marched herself to the door of the adjoining apartment. She planned to say cuttingly: "Is this perchance
your vine?" but when the door opened, all she got out
was a strangled, "Izzis . . . ?" What stunned her was

not her neighbor, whom she knew to be a bullet-headed man with thick glasses, but his foyer. It was full of mushrooms in flats on free-standing steel shelves as in libraries.

"Yes—s—s?" the neighbor said, and then saw what she was holding. "Aha," he cried, "my kudzu!"

"What*ever* it is," our girl said, recovering her voice and indignation, "I certainly don't want it in bed with me," and she thrust it at its owner.

"You haven't seen anything," the man said softly. "Let me show you."

What he showed her was a caution. As they passed through the foyer he explained that the mushrooms were there because he could keep it dark, and as she entered the living room she stumbled on something and would have gone down had she not grabbed a grapevine. What she stumbled on was a thick sheet of cork. The living room was paved with it. "Keeps the water from leaking through the ceiling below," her neighbor said briefly. "I had a lot of trouble with them down there."

"Say," she said, noticing what she still had hold of, "is this a *grape*vine?"

"Catawba," he said. "I'm really a vine specialist. The mushrooms in the foyer are pastime—a side shoot, you might say." He chortled hoarsely, and she edged away. "Careful," he said. "Poison ivy." She squeaked and leaped back to his side. The poison ivy was growing lushly from a wooden tub up a wooden pole that held on to the ceiling with a rubber suction cup. "My own invention," her neighbor said. "Loosen the suction cup, and you can wheel the vine around." She saw the tub had wheels she hadn't noticed. She thought of asking why anybody would ever want to wheel plants around, but decided she'd live happier without knowing.

Her neighbor named off several other specimens for her, pointing with a trowel since, except for narrow paths, the living room was pure jungle, and one plant looked pretty much like another to her. "Now this way, please," he said, striking out boldly. "Mind the *Clematis paniculata*."

"Where we going?" she asked, hurrying along to keep him in sight.

"Laboratory," he said from the side of his mouth. "Careful of the *Ampelopsis tricuspidata*."

"All I see's this Boston ivy," she mumbled, suddenly wondering about boa constrictors.

"That's it," he said, and plunged sharp left through a bower of wisteria into the bathroom. "Bathtub is the clinic," he said. "Ailing plants go there. And all these trays are for germination tests."

"What kind of tests?" she asked, sniffing hard; the place had a sour-mash smell.

"Seeds," he said as to a toddler. "Sprouting seeds."

She suddenly became aware of a buzzing in the air. It was caused by fruit flies spiraling up from trays he was uncovering. "Bugs!" she yipped, and decided to leave right away. He offered to start her off on a forest of her own with slips from anything he had, but she didn't encourage him. In fact she bought some 2, 4-D the very next day, just in case his kudzu vine got fresh again.

Another apartment-house gardener, a woman this time, was less methodical than the vine specialist and so had accumulated over the years a little bit of everything, running to some 193 items by the time I met her in San Francisco. She was just then moving into a one-room studio apartment situated on the ground floor. My wife and I were living on the floor above, and as the movers kept dragging in plants and spotting them around the entry and along the gangway we began laying small bets with each other on whether they'd find a place to put the next one or have to stand there holding it. Most things were in redwood planters, from a two-gallon size on up, and one was a magnolia grandiflora tree in a tub that took three men to tote and a fourth to steer them, like a coxswain.

We didn't get to stay till the end of the act, having to leave for an appointment, and when we returned, it was dark. We couldn't hear any moving men down below, though, so we assumed they had found places for all the plants. They had, too, and that night we got an inkling of what had happened toward the end of the job.

One of the features of the building was a fifteen-pound tomcat named Pushkin, who had a deceptively mild meow, since he was always spoiling for a fight. He conducted these fights at night with other neighborhood sports, and this night they started with the usual preliminary bouts in the gangway. But it was plain from the whoops of terror that Pushkin had a new advantage. He was, we found out later, climbing the new magnolia grandiflora and then dropping on his enemies' backs like an avenging angel as they sneaked along the passage.

His tour de force, however, came when his main rival, a huge black tom, showed up. This one always traveled by rooftop, and Pushkin regularly met him on the fire escape, a staircase that led from our bathroom window to the garden. The bouts usually lasted several minutes, but this night's fight was over almost as soon as it started. Apparently Pushkin merely dodged when the other jumped down from the roof at him, and let the black tom land in the middle of a dozen potted plants the movers had, no doubt in desperation, covered the steps of the fire escape with. The plants were varieties of cactus and were absolutely ferocious. When the black cat plunged into them he belted out a yowl that lasted for two blocks after he clawed his way out of the cacti and climbed up and down a telephone pole and a slow policeman who were in his way en route home.

The incident made Pushkin's reputation, so his owner, who also owned the building, decided to say nothing to the new tenant about violating the fire laws with her cactus collection on the escape. My wife and I didn't mind. The window that opened on the fire escape wouldn't go up more than six inches, we had found, and we would have had to soap ourselves to escape.

Chapter 18

NEIGHBORHOOD GARDEN OF VS.

A SEED company was holding a contest to see if any home gardener could discover a certain new color of marigold that might occur somewhere as a mutation. One day in came a letter from a woman in New England. "If you get some seeds from somebody in this town," she wrote darkly, "they will be mine. I was almost ready to pick them and send them to you, and my next-door neighbor stole them. I know she stole them because I saw her looking at them and now they are gone."

Just goes to show you how one gardener regards another when the chips are down. People who think gardeners are a jolly lot and as loyal toward each other as fraternity brothers don't know much about gardeners. Or fraternity brothers, for that matter.

In its quiet way, gardening is war. I can illustrate this nimbly with an item from a time when my wife and I had decided to live on a farm. The farm was in Missouri, our home state, and we had a big vegetable garden. My wife loved cucumbers, so she raised a big and very early crop the first year, surprising all the neighbors, whose cucumbers were nowhere near eating size yet. Beginner's luck, they thought. But when she then stated that she would have the first cucumbers of the season *every* year, a kind of low-level panic swept the countryside. Nobody minded our having a garden, but we were too new and too outlandish to shine at it. Immediately the other wives (women did 90 per cent of the gardening in a farm community, we found) threw caution to the winds and went to planting cucumbers the next spring far earlier than their common sense told them to. Where we lived, the last frost was due in mid-April on the average, and would you believe it, some of those women were seeding cucumbers on mild days in February. When they sprouted at all, they got frozen stiff in the next cold snap. Meanwhile my wife went humming along, smiling to herself, and two weeks before anybody had more than buttons on their cucumber vines, here she was again, playing Lady Bountiful with banana-sized cucumbers. (As a matter of fact, she gave *all* the early ones away, as if we had so many we were already sick and tired of them.)

The general opinion was that we had an invisible greenhouse, and my wife was willing to let everyone think so. Her system, as nearly as I could see (she didn't tell me much, either), involved some pre-soaking of seeds in a magic solution; early planting in the basement under a light bulb; outdoor plantings under glass, plastic, and waxed paper in various spots; and tender, loving care.

On this same farm, since I wasn't really farming, I did so much more gardening than the other men that their wives came to look on me with sharp distrust as a spy. Especially so when they were being too busy to keep their gardens spruced up. One time when we stopped by our nearest neighbors, the Gus Brinkmeyers, on some small errand, Daisy Brinkmeyer spotted me sauntering across the back yard, and instead of hello, what burst out was a screech: "Oh my God—there he goes to look at my garden!" She was right—it was a mess. Did me a world of good.

There has been a swing away from the first-of-the-season harvest in recent years, in favor of a vogue for the late-late produce. This brings out the very demon in most gardeners. True, a dissident gardener has occasionally said, "Personally, I'm tickled to death when fall comes and I can spend my weekends logging sofa time," but gardening will be undone if there is much of this kind of honesty.

Like the early-bird gardeners, the late birds must outwit nature, mainly by trying to take the bite out of the first frost or two. This leads to many a domestic disappearance from house to garden of heaters, fans, and assorted wraps. Flannel petticoats and camel-hair coats recruited from among the mothballs have come back into their own in some areas for this purpose, and shower curtains are so popular as covers for temporary coldframes that in certain sections of the country October is known semiofficially as "tub-baths-only" month. A male gardener almost got himself divorced one November when his wife found her electric blanket missing. He brought it back when she threatened to name his watermelon patch as correspondent.

Had the watermelon man got away with it, he might have succeeded in his ambition. He was trying for watermelon for Christmas dinner. His ambition, strictly speaking, was not watermelon for Christmas but the utter confusion of his brother-in-law, who was also a gardener and who had been driving him wild every Christmas by arriving with a wizened tomato he had just picked in the garden from his last surviving plant. The plant was enclosed in a pliofilm tent warmed by an electric light on an extension cord from the garage and ringed by a snow fence banked with straw.

Since gardening *is* war, it is well to be prepared with tactics. The following vest-pocket guide will be found invaluable. Any one of the following remarks, when aimed at an appropriate target, is guaranteed to explode:

Oh well, anything will grow in soil like this.

What are these supposed to be—potatoes?

This lettuce about two weeks old? Oh—two months?

You could save a lot of money buying this stuff at the grocery store.

Did you prune this spirea lately, or was there an accident?

With all these fancy tools it'd be a wonder if you *didn't* manage to grow something.

Chapter 19

THAT HARDY PERENNIAL,
THE WINTER GARDENER

AND since we were just talking of the late-late frost-covered gardener, perhaps we should at this point pin up on the specimen board the winter gardener himself. He is not the same as the late-late gardener and in fact would not thank you for even bringing the point up. He is a man (not many women in this club) whom that tired word "challenge" fits like a birthmark. Winter gardeners remind me of the Vermont farmer who got disgusted with rocky soil at last and moved to a fertile river-bottom farm in Iowa. After a few years he pulled up stakes again and came traipsing back to tough old Vermont. When they asked him why, his answer was considered very Vermonty: "Farmin' in Ioway's too dern easy," he said.

All gardeners are considered to some extent out of their minds by non-gardeners, but even summer gardeners call winter gardeners mad. "Here it was—a cold, gray day with a thin and bitter wind, and a sniff of snow in the air," one summer gardener muttered, "and the Strelands had asked us over for dinner. Streland's become a winter gardener, but it slipped my mind, and anyway, who would be thinking about gardening on a day like that?" Streland would, it turned out.

"We came up the front walk leaning into the wind," our summer gardener went on, "throats muffled up, ears brittle, and we could see the blazing log fire through the picture window, and Streland mixing hot buttered rums. Gad! But when he came to the door, we didn't even get to take off our wraps. Didn't even get to warm our hands at the fire. 'This way!' he said, and led a nonstop march right through the house, putting on his woolly cap and overcoat en route.

"Would you believe it, we spent the next forty minutes in his garden, visiting half-frozen parsnips and kale, peeping under straw thatches at shivering Swiss chard, cooing over coldframes chock-a-block with little bitty lettuces. And my wife—teetering over frozen clods in new thirty-dollar spike heels.

"And when we'd done our duty by the last leek and turnip and were mushing our way back to the house, we still had to go down to the cellar yet. There he's got him some witloof chicory roots in sand, sprouting French endive. 'Cost you $2.25 a pound in the market,' he says, only he hasn't got any to show us yet. 'Come back in two weeks.' Two weeks! Two years would be too soon."

Small wonder some people think winter gardeners are fiends in gardener's clothing. They do seem awfully keen on dragging one and all through their gardens, and the worse the day, the better they like it. However, if no one shows up, they'll drag themselves, which makes them as impartial as the very icy blasts they brave.

Perhaps this is the point to ask a question. What rewards does winter gardening offer? (And by the way, winter gardening in coastal California doesn't count. Or in parts of Florida and other such unfrosty places. It isn't fair if the climate cooperates.)

If you ask the typical winter gardener such a rash question, ask it in a cozy spot and be sitting in a comfortable chair. You'll be there quite a while, wondering why you ever turned him on.

He will cite and expand upon some or all of these points as reasons for winter-gardening:

> Vitamin C from fresh vegetables
> Muscle tone
> Flavor
> Menu variety
> Triumph over difficulties
> Horticultural curiosity
> Science
> Affection and sentiment
> Love of nature
> He-manliness
> Zen

There is still another reason he probably won't mention. It is the talking-dog reason. It gets its name from the story about the man who taught his dog to say

"Hello," "Well, well," and "Pass the biscuits." After a steady diet of these three remarks, the man's friends grew restive, and one was finally elected to tell him his dog's conversation was too limited for a very stimulating chat.

"Shucks," the man said, "you fellows miss the whole point. What the dog says don't matter. It's the *way* he says it!"

Chapter 20

THE HURRY-UP GARDENER

SOMETIMES when I think of my father in the garden all I see is a blur. He was so energetic a man, watching him for five minutes could wear you out for an hour. "Garden" is almost too fancy a word here. It was a back yard, and that's what we called it. It was in University City, a suburb of St. Louis, and in the old section where we lived, the tacit agreement was that nobody put up fences, so that all the back yards should merge to form a winding strip of park. This worked except when somebody got sore at a neighbor and slapped up a fence. I mention it because our yard did have a fence, along the back line, and it was there because Father's energy had got on the nerves of the man who lived in the adjoining property. Father thought he was some kind of a nut.

Mark Twain could have been talking about Father when he remarked, "Few things are harder to put up with than the annoyance of a good example." That was

certainly the effect he had on all the neighbors, especially
in springtime. At the first hint of softness in the air
he was outside pawing the earth, testing its dampness.
While neighbors watched sidelong and moodily through
windows, he rammed a stake here, a stake there, to tell
where certain new projects were to flower, strode rapidly
from plant to plant, appraising claims for survival and
ruthlessly condemning the sickly and the lazy. He was
off and speeding before his neighbors had even started
their motors. The wonder was they never lynched him.

Not in his wildest fancy did he consider growing
anything from seed except grass. He bought plants, and
he expected them to appreciate it and flourish. If they
didn't, they got yanked out. Once in a long while he gave
an unthrifty plant—they were usually roses; he was death
on roses— another chance, trying it somewhere else after
carrying it around by the neck like a skinny plucked
chicken. He was one of those people who can treat plants
rough and get away with it.

He did his pruning in the same hurry-up way. If in an
absent-minded moment he asked my brother Ted and me
to prune something, what frequently happened was that
as we were still looking the task over and holding a
gentlemanly debate on where to begin, Father came
charging by us, and whack-whack-whack, the job was
over, and forward to the next. Left to himself once, Ted
pruned a Paul's Scarlet climber by simply sawing it off
a foot from the ground, which was even worse than

Father would have done, and he had a fit when he saw it. The Paul's Scarlet bloomed better the following season than it ever had, and Father said he was glad Ted was catching on at last.

Needless to say, when it came to fertilizing, Father didn't have the patience to fool around with compost. It was far and away too slow. He did in some years order a load of manure, but it was too slow, too, and an old lady neighbor to the south made a point of wearing a clothespin on her nose when outside while the manure was still ambitious.

What Father relied on was chemical fertilizer, and he liked it strong, with big numbers on the bag. Half a cup of this dynamite was plenty for a rose bush, but he wanted them to get going, and he never stopped with a half cup. Sometimes he killed with kindness, but his fertilizing theory was winningly simple; he reasoned that if he were a rose bush he'd starve on a skimpy half cup of fertilizer; two or three cups were little enough, Lord knew.

One time a nature's-way advocate got hold of Father and tried to talk him into using ladybugs to curb aphis on his roses. The man knew where you could buy cold-storage ladybugs like so many jelly beans. Father watched a ladybug moseying around on a rose leaf for a while and then said it'd take her a week to get down to business at that rate, and maybe she had time to fritter, but he didn't.[1]

His idea of fighting bugs was to absolutely fog the yard with dust till you couldn't see across it. This of course fogged the neighborhood also, in whatever direction the wind was blowing, and automatically knocked off all the neighbors' bugs. The neighbors were not particularly grateful and often had a houseful of noxious dust before they could rush to close their windows. Consequently they were all rather happy one year when the wind changed as Father was booming out a cloud of rotenone powder, and blew it all back in his face. It raised such a ruckus with his sinuses that he had to give up dusting for the season, and this temporarily blunted his interest in gardening. He took a trip to Colorado instead, and for once the neighborhood was delighted to see him hurrying, as he loaded suitcases into his Buick sedan and zoomed off, sneezing.

[1] Science now is inclined to agree with him to some extent. Studies at the University of California's Berkeley Experiment Station have shown that when ladybugs are brought in by man they fly off home if it is spring, and are rather sluggish if released in summer. However, the home-grown ladybugs are rough on aphis, and also on such pests as scale insects, mealy bugs, and spider mites.

Chapter 21

GARDENERS ARE SCOUNDRELS

A BRITISH woman gardener, transplanted to the United States, was making a trip back to the old country. "If you wish me ever to smile again, Etheldreth," said her old mother as she was about to leave, "do not fail to return with cuttings of Cox's Orange Pippin."

"I shall endeavor my utmost, Mum," said the daughter, "even though I surmise it is against the statutes, and I may go to gaol for it."

Cox's Orange Pippin, unknown to most Americans, is a popular dessert apple in England. Well, back came our British gardener in due time from her journey and faced the United States customs sleuths calmly. They looked her over, saw nothing suspicious, waved her along. Little did they know of gardeners' guile.

Arriving home, she removed her innocent-looking hat trimmed with flowers and began removing the flowers and handing their stems to her mother. "Pippin cuttings," she remarked. She then opened a pencil box and

99

took out the pencils. "Ignore the pointed ends, please," she said. Yes, Pippin cuttings. But she was not through. Unwinding her corset, she began pulling out every other stay. "*More* Cox's Orange Pippins, for mercy sakes?" cried her mother, and they were. Those of the cuttings not exhausted from travel were planted, and the survivors grew into trees that are bearing fruit to this very day.

Needless to say—needless at least to other gardeners—neither mother nor daughter ever had any qualms over the smuggling. This is absolutely typical of gardeners everywhere. At heart they are simple pirates all when it comes to plant propagation.[1]

Like other pirates, gardeners don't spend much time being sorry for their sins. Some of them are brazen about it and have the audacity to make up rules that say it is their duty to help themselves to anything loose because they are being nature's handmaidens.

I know a woman gardener who got to noticing a dogwood tree growing wild among some other roadside things along a country lane she often drove on her way to shop. To do her justice, she had an idea that nobody would care if she liberated the dogwood, and she said she thought nobody owned the land it was on. And if any-

---

[1] Some gardeners include manure as another thing they have a perfect right to. They swipe it from farms if they can, and their reasoning is curious. First they'll tell you they don't take enough to make any difference to the owner anyway. If this doesn't go down, they look you in the eye and say: "Well, *I* appreciate manure!"

body did, she added, it would be just like them to burn off the brush some fine day and kill her tree. The only thing that had kept her from taking it was a distaste for doing it in plain sight of a certain tobacco-chewing character who lived across the road.

Well, one day he wasn't in his yard as she passed, so she stopped the car, grabbed up a spade she had been carrying in the back seat for weeks, and went to work. She got it dug, but the tree turned out to be bigger than she'd thought and almost impossible to jam into the car trunk. As she was trying to bend it into a kind of pretzel, along comes Mr. Chewing Tobacco. She could have died. But, "Ptooie," says he, "can I help you with that thing, ma'am?" And he did. Got out a plug-tobacco jackknife and cut off enough branches to let the dogwood fit the trunk. "That'll be two dollars, please," he then said. "No charge for the labor." (This was in 1956, and I suppose he'd have to get more today.)

"You mean you own this land?" she cried.

"Who did you think owned it, lady?" he said.

She forked over the two dollars and simmered on home with her tree. "That thing'll never live," her husband said, the minute he saw it. "When will you learn that just because something's free doesn't mean it's any good?" He was half right—the dogwood didn't live.

I am not, by the way, implying that male gardeners are saints, or even that they are necessarily a minority among horticultural kleptomaniacs. It just happens that I know more light-fingered women than men. And in some cases these girls have even chosen to loot by proxy, making their men do it for them, scruples or no. One woman gardener of my acquaintance even got a dog, to lend an innocent air when she strolled around the neighborhood casing the gardens. She would then bring her husband, and while she and the dog covered for him, the poor guy would have to reach through fences and snap off cuttings she coveted.

Another girl gardener, still in her early twenties and engaged to a young man whose hobby was not gardening but photography, talked him into taking her to a flower show at the Arena in St. Louis. She said it would be a stunning chance for some color shots.

It was, and he had taken twenty-five or thirty exposures on his roll of film when she made a strange request of him. "Would you lie down on your stomach, please, Harold, and wiggle under this trellis thing," she asked, "and pinch me off a little smidgin of that heavenly pink-and-white Belgian azalea in that formal-garden display on the other side?"

"Awrk—k—k—k?" said Harold, swallowing hard.

"I'll hold your little camera," she said, taking his Leica from him and giving him a push toward the trellis.

Well, it worked out into a fiasco all around. When he arrived under the trellis flat on his belly, he found himself looking into the face of an outraged exhibitor and had to back up quick, carrying an azalea twig in his teeth. The exhibitor came boiling after him, and in the uproar his fiancée scampered off to avoid the scene. When he finally located her, in the Italian Garden, and handed over the dad-gummed azalea, it wasn't the right one. "And I lost that old camera of yours," she complained. "I looked *everywhere*, but the silly thing is so little. Anyway, I'll buy you a nice big box Brownie for your next birthday."

You'd think he would have broken the engagement after that, but he didn't. He said his fiancée was impossible, but at least life with her wouldn't be flat, and he could always rest up in the darkroom.

Chapter 22

DICTATOR FOR HIRE

IF YOU are one of us who usually can't afford to hire a gardener, you'll love this chapter. A hired gardener isn't all skittles and beer. In fact you sometimes wonder—after talking to someone who does have a gardener—how gardeners manage to find employment at all instead of being in the lordly position of saying, "I can give you half a day every other week except when the salmon are running, during the Kentucky Derby, and when I take the family to Bermuda."

A woman I know, we'll call her Ella, had this nervous tic that came on her every Monday morning. She couldn't sit still and as she was about to go lurching off to see a psychiatrist, her husband handed her the answer on a silver platter. "It's nothing but that blinking George," he said. "He's got you buffaloed." George was the gardener, and Monday was his day at their place, and if Ella had told her husband once, she had told him a thousand times: "I never have any bloom." The reason she didn't was that George didn't believe in flowers. He said they sapped a plant's energy.[1] The result was, if this poor woman wanted a few flowers from her garden for a little party on, say, Thursday, she had to hotfoot it outside and snatch up whatever she could find no later than sunup Monday morning, before the gardener got to them. Of course by Thursday the bouquet might not be in much of a party mood. Once, when she had tried to get the gardener to let her flowers alone, he had said in effect that it might be her yard, but it was his reputation, and anybody who paid him for know-how was by gosh going to get know-how.

Some people find that having a hired gardener is too exhausting, and they can't do a lick of work for a day or two after. "Keeps me busy just following him around picking up things," one woman said. "Pruners, spades, spray, dibble—it's like playing drop-the-handkerchief every Wednesday. In fact he does drop his handkerchief occasionally."

Others find it wears them out to have a professional gardener because of their feeling they must keep him busy. "Every time he stops to scratch," said one client of a woolly-shirted gardener, "I figure it costs me a

[1] As a matter of fact, they do. Obeying nature's law, the plant's mission in life is to go to seed—an annual plant's farewell act. Since flowering is the prelude to seeding, if you keep the flowers picked, the plant can't wear itself out going to seed. However, the important thing is to pick the flowers simply before they go to seed—not to pick them while they are still mere buds.

nickel." Actually, nobody has to worry about there being enough to keep the gardener busy even in a small garden. One of the wonders of a garden is the way it can soak up labor and hardly show it. This is also one of the sorrows of a hired gardener's life; they have their troubles too. "What have you been doing all day?" is a question that can set a hired gardener vibrating like a tuning fork.

Too many such questions may cause the gardener to raise his price, his rate structure being a strangely argued thing at best, and swayed by such elements as how much his feet hurt, the size of his wife's beauty bill, and the prevailing wind. One hired gardener who charged thirty-five cents an hour more than his client had paid a previous one appeared to base this on having learned his business under a local nurseryman of excellent repute. It was "Mr. Wilson and me always did it this way," and "Mr. Wilson and me never lost a plant," until finally the client ran into Mr. Wilson one day and mentioned it. "Ferguson?" said the nurseryman. "Oh, yes—Ferguson. Very good man. Worked for me one afternoon three years ago during the Easter rush."

Another one's price shot up all of a sudden when he found that one of the houses where he gardened was being pictured in a home magazine. After that he drove carloads of friends slowly by the place on weekends, pointing it out as one of his houses. The owners got the rate boost the same as all his other customers.

If this sounds as if the gardener here was a snob, there is no need for surprise. Hired gardeners are apt to be snobs. They may be snobbish toward those who hire them (regarding them as poor seconds to wealthier clients), and also toward those who don't ("Too cheap, huh?"), with little runs and trills of snobbery in between. A hired gardener who spots one of his clients in the newspaper society section immediately becomes more patronizing toward his less favored customers, and anyone who hires a gardener who also gardens for the president of the local bank is unlikely to rise above fourth grade in the gardener's esteem.[2]

Hired gardeners are also as aware of other prestige hash marks as a junior executive. Here's what happened in a Chicago suburb: The same gardener worked for two families next door to each other. Both the husbands were vice presidents of companies, one of a three-hundred-million-dollar corporation and the other of a five-hundred-million-dollar one. On the days this gardener was working on the three-hundred-million-dollar side he kept an eye on the other place, and when *that* vice president rolled his Cadillac out of the garage to go to work, the gardener hurried over to dust off the windshield and speak a pleasant word to the five-hundred-million-dollar fellow. All this on the other man's time. And if you think he did the same for the three-hundred-million-dollar man's Lincoln convertible when working next door, try again.

But at least that hired gardener worked, even if he did work illegally for the opposition part of the time, but

---

[2] Presidents of small-town banks, as a class, have proportionately more gardeners among them than any other occupational group except doctors, if you can believe a market survey made a few years ago.

I know of another one in a class by himself. He was a very elderly man who had a kind of life tenure in return for gardening and caretaking on a country place a friend of mine bought in the Deep South for weekend relaxing. The new owner was happy to find that his tenant talked knowingly of the climate, saying that gardening there was strictly a job for one experienced with the weather, and the owner began looking forward to soon hauling great carloads of his tenant's home-grown vegetables back to the city every weekend.

Spring came and the tenant moved his rocking chair out onto his porch and told the owner: "Too early to plant yet," whenever he asked, which he did so often that his wife asked him for heaven's sake to stop pestering the poor old man. He stopped for a couple of weeks, and then his resistance broke and he again asked the tenant when he was going to start the garden. "Oh, much too hot to plant right now," the old boy told him, rocking contentedly. "Weather done changed on us."

The owner was new to this southern climate, so he kept waiting for a cool spell and kept on eating limp store vegetables, until along about September impatience got the best of him again, and he looked up his tenant, who was still rocking. "Too late for any plantin' now," the tenant chuckled, shaking his head. "Like I said, gardening here takes plenty knowin'." After he had thought this remark over, the owner decided it was so right that it was brilliant, and he got rid of the place—lock, stock, and tenant.

Chapter 23

MULCH ADO

ASK any ten gardeners the purpose of mulching, and you stand a good chance of getting ten different answers. To make it still more confusing, all ten may be right.

My dictionary doesn't waste much time on mulch. "Straw, leaves, loose earth, etc.," it says, as if any clod ought to know *that*, "spread on the ground or produced by tillage to protect the roots of newly planted trees, crops, etc." No mention of non-newly-planted things. As a sop it adds that the word mulch traces back to the Middle English word for soft, *molsh*, and earlier from the Old English *mylisc*, for mellow. Gardening can be mighty educational.[1]

Mulch may not be a plant's best friend, but it is a good runner-up. Even though my dictionary doesn't admit it,

[1] There are people who mulch with rocks. Some joke on them that mulch means "soft" in Middle English!

a mulch's main job is to keep water in the soil, where plants can use it. Would you believe that this is even more important in wet climates than in dry ones? Sure is. This is because the earth acts as a wick, drawing moisture up to the surface, where it evaporates. In a dry climate the surface earth dries out and stops this evaporation, but in a moist climate, where it doesn't, the soil can lose water faster than rain can replace it. A mulch will put a stop to this rapid loss because water can't travel upward through mulch very well, so it stays in the ground.

If you are wondering whether that dried-out top layer of earth in the dry climate needs any mulch—since it is already controlling evaporation without it—the answer is that it could use some to help protect plant roots from extreme temperature changes, another job mulch does. Mulch enthusiasts are like insurance salesmen—they never think you can have enough.

Some gardeners go in for deep mulching—that is, deeper than a couple of inches, say. Deep mulching acts on these gardeners as does whisky; they can get looped on it, and some deep-deep mulchers pile the stuff on until a row of plants with mulch on each side looks like a line of soldiers peeping out of a trench. These enthusiasts will make as if to hit you if you scorn their system. For some reason they assume that what works for them in their climate and location will work anywhere, just like long division or holy wedlock.

Well, at least one laboratory test[2] on three kinds of soils showed that in the case of sandy loam, by increasing the depth of mulch, a point of diminishing returns was reached, resulting in an *increase* of water loss by evaporation. Nobody, including the laboratory experimenters, claimed that this absolutely proved anything, though; except, perhaps, that you can't be sure you know all the answers.

If anyone thinks from what's been going on here that I'm dead against deep mulching personally, you ought to see my garden. Actually, you *can't* see it for the mulch, in some places. If you fell down there, you'd just bounce. But lots of things make a difference in how you can mulch—such as season, crop, soil, pests, and so on. Sometimes a garden can make a woman seem almost easy to please.

Gardeners who mulch with stuff they bring to the garden—compost, peatmoss, sawdust, and so on—often look unkindly at those who get along with nothing but a dust mulch. The dust mulchers reply that in addition to a much neater garden, they get the same results so far as stopping water loss is concerned, and also they get more cultivation. The cultivation point is one of those sticky ones. "Cuts feeder roots," you'll hear. It's hard work too. On the other hand, cultivation helps bacteria thrive,

[2] Cited by Professor Firman E. Bear of Rutgers University in his *Soils and Fertilizers*, John Wiley & Sons, Inc., New York, 1942, a down-to-earth text. There—I said it, and I'm glad.

and good bacteria help plants. Bacteria are so tiny, by the way, there can be two million of them in a teaspoonful of rich garden soil without their crowding each other. Population explosion is old stuff to bacteria. But in a poor soil there may be only a single bacteria for every thousand in the rich soil.

There are gardeners who think the sort of mulch used affects the flavor of the produce. For instance, branches of conifers are favored by certain strawberry growers. My wife and I gave this a whirl once, using branches of red cedar (*Juniperus virginiana*) in a big strawberry patch we had in Missouri. Oh, well, it did make an attractive mulch, and impressed visitors. One of them thought it was a lawn, and walked right through the strawberries.

A gardener I know says she'd love to use mulch but can't because it attracts termites. I've found lots of things under mulch, including pens and pocket knives I had lost, but so far no termites. However, I'm still looking. I knew another woman gardener who grew so desperate for mulch one thin year that she used some old hooked rugs from the attic. It made a weird-looking garden, but she said it was lovely to walk on barefoot.

Chapter 24

EXPERTS, FAKE AND OTHERWISE

THE telephone rang, and it was Long Distance from San Francisco about a television show. "Say," I said to my wife. "Man here wants us to be on his show, 'The Experts,' to give advice on gardening."

"He must have the wrong number," she said.

I shook my head. "Says he read the book."

"Then he couldn't have read it very *well*," she said, "or he'd know we didn't claim to be the authorities."

We said no, thanks, to the show, but ducking friends and neighbors was not so easy. Simply because we had happened to do a book about gardening experts and their know-how,[1] everybody we knew and some we didn't had elected us experts on gardening. "I suppose," my wife said, "if we did a thing on surgeons, everyone would expect us to take his appendix out."

It was true that we knew our way around a garden and had years of experience wondering why things didn't

[1] *Garden to Order*, Doubleday & Company, Garden City, New York, 1963. The experts in this case were Burpee seedsmen.

113

grow in various climates. We considered ourselves good practical gardeners, with the scars to prove it, and to tell the truth, we didn't want to be called experts. It was our experience that you could define an expert as someone who didn't quite agree with other experts. But people, we found, believe what they want to believe, and they wanted to believe we knew all the answers to all their horticultural complaints.

Sometimes it was easy. "You call this a healthy parsley plant?" a neighbor demanded of my wife the other day, about a specimen she had asked advice on. Pat tasted a leaf. "No, I'd call it a sickly chervil plant," she said.

Another time, as we were sitting down to dinner, a neighbor strode in waving an artichoke plant threateningly. "What's the matter with it?" he asked.

"It's dead," I said after a brief examination, "and you're dropping leaves in the soup."

"I know it's dead," he said, "but what's it dead *from?* You're garden experts, so cough up."

If you imagine it does the least good to spell the whole thing out again—we never claimed, etc.—don't. It doesn't. Another fellow woke me up one morning knocking at the back door with what seemed to be his head. It was a potted fern, and he wished to know how you tell if a pot plant is pot-bound. A good heavy potted plant in your hands can be an almost overwhelming temptation in a case such as this.[2]

---

[2] By the way, speaking of pot plants, haven't you sometimes wondered how some old broomstick of a plant can live along

After a lot of geeing and hawing we finally found that there is only one thing that will satisfy a gardener who has a question, and that is an answer. ("I don't know," isn't an answer, incidentally.)

We now give one of three kinds of answers to each and every question:

1. The right one if we happen to know it.
2. The same thing if we don't know it but have time to find out.
3. A wild guess if we're cornered and can't stall for time.

The system is working much better than when we tried denying we were experts. We find that our most popular answers, by five to one, are the wild guesses. The wilder the better.

---

for years in a handful of the same old earth? Well, it seems that of all the food a green plant needs, less than one-tenth comes from the soil. The rest it gets from the air. So the experts claim, as least, and have for the past 150 years.

Chapter 25

THE GREEN TRAP

A FAMILY I know used to have a month-long visitation every now and then from the husband's elder sister, and at the end of it there wouldn't be an uncracked bowl left in the house. She had a habit of sticking the bowls in the oven and forgetting about them. "Cheap stuff," she'd say when they cracked. I'm not sure of why she put them in the oven though I think she thought any old bowl should double as a casserole. Finally they hit on a scheme to keep the old dragon away. They put in a garden. The very next time she descended on them they hustled her out to the garden and pressed a scuffle hoe in her hands. "From now on you're going to take it good and easy while you're here, Auntie," they cried. "Nothing but healthful outdoor air and sunshine. Would you rather weed the onions or the beans first?" She made a few swipes at the onions, and the next day she left.

Of course this was a special case of the garden as persuader. Usually the garden is there first, and the idea of putting guests to work in it comes as a happy after-thought. Comes, that is, to those gardeners who work their guests. Not all do, and some who don't are as touchy even about guests watching *them* work as a pickpocket with a hangnail.

This type of gardener is not nearly so plentiful, though, as the work-'em-till-they-drop type. One of the latter had a farm close to our farm when we used to have a farm, only his was a weekend place. It was a mighty primitive weekend place, too, just about as it had been half a century before, when its log house was built. No electricity, no running water. Just a spring you dipped from. Well, wouldn't you know, with a system like that he went and put in a big garden a good hundred feet uphill from the spring, and the next time a dry spell hit, he wore himself skinny the following weekend toting water by the bucketful uphill from spring to garden.

But once was enough. He pranced right out and bought himself a dozen or so buckets, and next dry spell he threw an old-fashioned house party at the place and organized an old-fashioned bucket brigade. If you've ever been in a bucket brigade you know that once it gets going, it's like a parachute—you just about have to stay with it for the duration. So our neighbor got his garden good and soaked. It was a dry year, and we noticed that he had a different crowd each house party. He ran through something like sixty guests that summer, and never had better tomatoes, he told us.

My wife and I were not in any of his bucket brigades,

not because he didn't ask us but because by then we knew enough to take a walk. We had learned our lesson three years before. We were living then in midtown Manhattan and didn't have so much as a window box in our apartment, so when we were invited to spend one weekend in a part-time country home in Connecticut there was no holding us.

I picked up a tasteful plaid jacket with leather buttons at Brooks Brothers to go with some pants I already owned, and Pat outfitted herself in whatever Peck & Peck thought fit for a grouse-and-moors setting, which was her best guess at what she'd need. Very tweedy.

We bought an enormous wooden salad bowl for our hostess and went railroading up on the New Haven Friday evening, cheery as grigs. The salad bowl was a howling success. "How did you know I had a garden?" our hostess cried. "I've been dying for a huge big salad bowl, my dears."

It wasn't all she'd been dying for. Turned out her hired man had expired or graduated or something that spring, and the garden hadn't had a real good lick done on it since. This was midsummer. "I—uh—" said our hostess the next morning (a lone maiden lady, by the way, with executive qualities), studying my new plaid jacket and practically new pants. "I wonder if Jeem's things would fit you?"

What's the matter with what I have on, I thought. And Jeems who? Jeems the ex-hired man, that was who. And it was his overalls she had in mind. They were still hanging on a nail behind the toolhouse door, where a mouse had made a nest in one pocket. I changed my plans for a fresh-air stroll about the countryside, and got into the overalls as the mouse got out. I wasn't as reluctant as this probably sounds; the stroll could wait an hour while I got in a spurt of the kind of exercise I wasn't getting in the city. I selected a hoe in the toolhouse, ran a file over the edge, and asked the lady where the garden was.

"Right there," she said, pointing to a jungle as high as my head. "The weeds got a little ahead of me the last few weekends."

I put the hoe back and got a scythe, and spat on my hands for luck. . . .

"Weeding can get so monotonous," said my hostess at midmorning. Haying, she should have said. "Would you like to mow the lawn for a rest?" I mowed the lawn until noon. Until lunchtime, I almost said, but that would be exaggerating. I had a harvest hand's appetite by then, and Pat was a close second, having spent the morning in an old house dress the hostess had loaned her, excavating the shrubbery borders on the south and west sides of the house.

For lunch we all three sat at the kitchen table and gorged ourselves on crackers and a can of tuna. I thought we were having hors d'oeuvres until the hostess stacked the dishes in the sink and led the way back outside at a trot. "I hate to stop gardening for anything," she said. "There's never time enough."

In the afternoon I pruned the dooryard lilacs, which had been needing it since the Hoover administration, and took a few more turns at the garden, mostly to wolf raw carrots. I slipped a couple to Pat, who was doing the north and east shrubbery borders and seemed to be talking to herself. "Where is she?" I asked her. "Fixing dinner, I pray."

Just then our hostess came around the corner of the house with a spade and asked if I thought it was a good spade for transplanting. She got a much better answer than she might have got, by remarking immediately that she had something in the oven and couldn't stay away, but she could show me the transplanting she was talking about.

It was on a piece of acreage across the road, and involved some more lilacs. She was crazy about lilacs. She wanted three of them, as wide as automobiles, moved. Pat had come along to see what she was up to, and stayed to help transplant. We moved two of the lilacs in the daylight remaining, while our hostess hostessed in the kitchen.

"Lunch is probably their lightest meal here," I said. "Just a token. She's probably in there fixing an enormous New England boiled dinner now, or a standing rib roast, or a saddle of . . ."

"Let's hurry," Pat said, starting for the house at a desperate pace, "or I won't make it. I could eat a horse."

She wasn't offered horse. Tongue is what we had, cold tongue sliced thinly so everybody could have a piece. Cold tongue and baked beans. The beans were what had been in the oven. Dessert came as an after-thought—a jar of peaches put up the summer before and partly used up the weekend before we arrived. They were fizzing a bit, so she spooned off the top layer and served the rest. Of course we ate them. We would have eaten the top layer too if she hadn't put it out of our reach.

We spent the night but didn't stay for the next day's organized sport. And now, if I were making this up, I'd end this story by saying we set the house on fire or something as we left. The fact is, our hostess got off scot-free, but me, I began to tender up on the trip back to New York, and by Monday morning I had a roaring case of poison ivy, as bad as I ever had in my life. Riding the rush-hour subway downtown and back for a week while puffed till your seams are straining is a wonderful way to cure yourself of getting trapped in a work-hungry gardener's garden for a weekend, in case malnutrition isn't enough.

Chapter 26

WHERE WERE YOU LAST WEEK?

IT SEEMS to be a melancholy characteristic of gardeners that there is no pleasing them. I mentioned once before that my wife and I had put in a spell on a straightforward gardening book in which the know-how came from gardening experts we quizzed and quoted. Well, during the leg work on this job we visited some enormous farms where they were growing flowers for seed. It was like walking through acres of jewels alive, but do you know what these flower growers said? They said we should have been there last week, that's what they said. "These snapdragons are just a little past their prime . . . the verbena was much better several days ago . . . too bad you couldn't have got here when the petunias were at their peak." In a way it was heartening to find out that these professionals were as bad as the rest of us.

We once lived in a kind of French pension, only it was in the United States, and from the balcony of our second-floor teensy we gazed down upon a tiny garden chock-full of things. It was so chock-full even the bugs were crowded—a tree peony, parrot tulips, oxylis, azaleas, hydrangeas, nandinas, camellias, irises, espaliered apple and plum trees, a Seville orange so discouraged that it was ripening still marble-sized fruits, bamboo, and a passiflora vine climbing a utility-pole guy wire and preparing to throttle the service one day and probably electrocute us all, I was thinking. There were a lot more things in the garden, too, so there was always something blooming, but the landlady, Miss Eugenia, refused to be comforted. Always we had missed the best. You'd think this would have changed after we had been there long enough to have seen practically everything in bloom, wouldn't you? Ha! "The tree peony isn't a scrap as good this year as last," our Miss Eugenia would mourn, and if we happened to remark on how well the irises looked from our perch, there came an anxious inquiry of whether we had looked at them at seven o'clock that morning. At seven o'clock we had been looking at some bacon and eggs. "Ah," she would say, "at seven they *were* superb."

A rather deaf male neighbor of hers, the other side of a bristling, solid board fence, was also a gardener; specialty—carnations. He and I struck up a yelling acquaintance, and once I noticed from our balcony that a bed of his pink carnations was worth a compliment, so I roared one down to him and asked if he had raised them from seed or from plants in flats. "Yes—cats," he bawled back. "Every time I get some nice bloom, damn' cats get in here and dig. Too bad you didn't see these before they got to them." Sure enough, soon after he left, I watched a black-and-white tomcat climb the fence and hurry into the garden, as though he had been listening. He jostled no fewer than two carnations, stamping around in there, and in friendship's name I hurled a stale English muffin from the balcony at him, nipping off three blossoms he got blamed for the next day.

If you live in a climate where citrus flourishes, you can do as a friend of mine on the Mississippi gulf coast does. When his satsuma orange trees and his lemon tree ripen their fruit, there the fruit stays. If you visit him in the late fall, you get to stand in front of the trees and admire the yield, as it is tenacious about clinging and keeps on looking good. *He* never has to say you should have seen these lemons or oranges last week. They looked just the same last week as this week and will look the same next week, too.

A brash child visitor once grabbed off an orange. My friend turned a sickly green, and the mother, who could have sunk into the earth, wanted to paste the orange back on. "Oranges," the urchin declared, "are to eat," and the owner, smiling gamely, told him to go ahead and eat it. Turned out it had gone gooey inside, and the child made a horrible face and spewed it out. That put a damper on the viewing, and the party broke up. (Memo to child: Where were you a month or two before?)

I almost forgot—there is a type of gardener who is a

twist on the type I have been talking about. He doesn't tell you you should have seen the place last week—he tells you what it is going to be like *next year*. If you pause to admire the lilies or daisies or rhubarb, he yanks you along by the arm: "Well, all this is going to be changed. Now—let me show you." And he hauls out a plan of the garden-to-be. Or draws one on the ground with a stick. Or stands on a slight eminence such as the compost pile and points to where things are to go when he tears out what is there now.

I know still another gardener who is uniquely free of both the it-was-better-last-week lament and the wait-till-next-year one. We'll call her Lucille. She has executive ability the way dogs have fleas, and when she joined the garden club they elected her president so fast that for months she had to keep on introducing herself to irregular attenders of meetings. Lucille has a garden, of course, but she knows perfectly well where her talents lie. In fact you can even test her, just for fun, with a remark such as: "Lucille, I'll bet this gladiolus must really have been something last week, eh?" And Lucille, bless her heart, will give the glad a surprised look and say: "To tell you the honest truth, I just didn't notice. Fact is, I can't garden worth a hoot. But darling—can I *organize!*"

Chapter 27

H——! STANDS FOR HERB

A GARDENER who can take cucumbers or let them alone, or take endive or let it alone, and no hard feelings afterward, may get all gassed up if you say "herbs" to him. Another thing—it is the men gardeners who are so affected. Say "herbs" to a woman gardener, and if she isn't already raising some of them, at least she won't bite your head off and will probably leap at this tempting bait.

The trouble with these herbophobe males is that they think herbs are sissy. A woman married to one had better keep it quiet if she decides to have a whirl at seasoning with herbs. He'll make a face no matter what the food tastes like, and may just fill up on bread and be a martyr all evening. However, if he happens to discover a herb or two for himself, such as rosemary rubbed on lamb chops before he grills them over the charcoal, that's entirely different, and you'll never hear the end of it.[1]

[1] Rosemary is all wound up in ancient arcana. It stands for friendship, and figured in ceremonies, weddings and funerals

126

By the way, you might tell him that in France they think that one herb, sweet basil, won't grow if you don't cuss it out when planting the seed.

Maybe we should have started this study hour by saying what a herb is. This can snarl things up so amazingly when you get persnickety about it that let's just say a herb is a usually non-woody plant valued for its scent, flavor, or medicinal qualities. That covers most cases, and now we can forget all about it.

Oh, there's another bit of academism we'd better mention. It is the silent aitch versus the forthright aitch. One timid gardener who longs to grow herbs has never planted any because, she admitted, "I've never been sure about that aitch, so by not planting any—uh—any of them, I don't have to say the word." Others only a little less timid wait until they hear how you say it and then follow suit. I knew one gardener who always felt a little ashamed of her friends who didn't have enough bringing-up to say "erb" until one day she collided with a cast-iron character who snorted: "That's a lot of cockney nonsense. Listen: 'Erbert, bring mum 'er 'erbs over 'ere.' *That's* how that whole 'erb' business got started." That's how it ended, too, for that particular gardener.

Herbs were another of those things they were always scattering on the floor in medieval days. The lackeys

---

among them. It was also supposed to be good for rheumatism, heart trouble, weak eyes, and spots on the skin, to name a few. Some people think that smelling rosemary keeps you young.

curled up and slept on them at night, and could do the house cleaning with a hay rake when the place was due for a fresh mulching to make it smell better.

For the same purpose, and also as a touch of showmanship, men who were called court strewers preceded royal processions through a city, strewing sweet-smelling herbs. This was still going on here and there in Europe into the nineteenth century, and you can imagine what the streets smelled like on days royalty wasn't expected.[2]

Gardeners who shy away from growing herbs because they feel uncomfortable around those who keep talking about their herb gardens should jolly well live their own lives and plant herbs any old place. We used to raise a scandalous lot of tomatoes, and I planted sweet basil near them just to smell it while hacking at the everlasting weeds among the tomatoes. Other herbs got stuck in wherever there was room. Early Dutch settlers in America even planted chives in pastures. However, their idea was so the cows would **give** chives-flavored milk. This sounds pretty loony to me because we used to get terrible-tasting milk flavored with wild onions when our own cows could find them in the pastures. They were insane about them. Speaking of herbs in colonial times, dill seed was popular for eating in church. It helped people stand

---

[2] The strewing herbs included balm, rosemary, lavender, hyssop, sage, mints, thyme, marjoram. Souvenir hunters grabbing for sprigs ran the risk of having the king's horses step on their fingers but this crushing also helped release the herbs' fragrance.

the long-winded sermons, even if they did taste a little like dill pickles when they got out.

When a gardener likes tarragon, he really likes it. This herb brings out the zealot in people, maybe because it is pesky to grow. You can't find seed easily or sprout it easily if you do, so plants or cuttings are the usual means of propagation. And then, after you get them, they are likely to go poking along never amounting to anything and dying if you give them a harsh word.

I know exactly one gardener whose tarragon grows well. He never misses a chance to say something nice about it in its presence, and he isn't pretending. He is a superb cook with palate to match, and so speaks with authority. I am not trying to make a case for anything, but I'll tell you this: his tarragon is stuck in a cramped spot between a wall and a brick walk, and it grows like a noxious weed.

I might have said it grows like borage. If borage likes the climate, the way it grows is depressing to weeds. Here in north-central coastal California borage thinks it owns the earth. A plant that escaped our garden went in business for itself on the slope of the mountainside just below and started flinging seeds all over. Its children and grandchildren and great-grandchildren are now a wild all-borage garden, and one day, I suppose, they will blanket the Santa Lucia Range with little blue flowers. Some gardeners grow borage just for the sake of these

flowers, and others grow it to favor the bees, who are
devoted to it. An ancient couplet about borage goes:

I, Borage,
Bring alwaeis courage.

Like children, herbs are into everything. Take the
mints. They are good not only for juleps and sauce (the
English call spearmint "lamb mint"), but a sprig of a
mint will keep mice away, according to mint admirers.
Fennel dried and powdered is supposed to keep flies
away, as is a fresh bouquet of hyssop. Dried camomile
flowers brewed in boiling water make a liquid sleeping
pill.

Borage roots are used to color candy red, and drinking
red wine with sage leaves crushed in it was said to
sharpen the memory. Pour boiling water over coriander
seeds, and you have a drink that helps digestion. Pour
the boiling water over dried flowers of feverfew, and you
have a headache cure. If you need a hand cleaner and
an inkspot and rust remover, sorrel leaves are said to be
good (and, in the opinion of quite a few gardeners,
that's about all they *are* good for, if they're good for
that).

Perhaps one of the more bemusing uses of herbs is
the olden recommendation that you apply powdered
parsley seed to your head. Done three times a year, they
do say it keeps the hair from falling out. Looks something
like dandruff, too.

Chapter 28

ALL WORK AND A YARD WIDE

M Y WIFE and I plunged into married life charged with the care of a neglected yard lying in wait for somebody, anybody. We didn't know then that, like a new baby, a yard clamored for food, water, and coddling, not to mention leaf raking and snow shoveling in season, which no baby seemed to need. We had rented a house on a big lot in the St. Louis suburbs because our dog, a clumsy animal named Socks, took space. The lot seemed half a mile deep, most of it back yard. At first, while the dog did his running back there, we spent all our time inside, making friends with the furnace and the plumbing, and repainting the walls in dazzling colors. The painting was our own idea. The owner of the house, a timid little woman, dropped in now and then and spent the visits staring at our redecorating with her mouth slightly ajar. We served her coffee and cookies and assumed she was speechless with delight.

As the first spring came creeping over the countryside, my bride began growing fidgety about the front yard.

It was a sorry-looking patch in full view of the living-room windows. A nice lawn, she seemed to think, was the foundation of a happy marriage.

I had never built a lawn, so I paid a call on the neighborhood hardware store and returned bolstered with fertilizer, lime, grass seed, spade, rake, and advice. "Everything but the dynamite," I said after I had tried digging.

"I understand that the last family here had three children," my wife said, "and I suppose this is where they played." Apparently they had been two hundred-pound children, playing at Indian stomping games. It took a solid week of spare-time work to get even a so-so seedbed made. "And now you'll need a fence so people won't step on it," my wife said.

I saw no reason why they'd step on it, since there was a nice concrete part up the middle, but the mailman cut corners, the paper boy pioneered a cater-cornered trail, and the milkman sank in up to his ugly ankles after I watered. I threw up a rope-and-broomstick fence which the same milkman fell over the very next day and then warned us that his brother-in-law was attending law school at night.

In spite of this, the front yard began to green up, and we admired it from the front porch until we were snapped to attention by a remark from next door. We happened to overhear our neighbor's twin boys asking Pop if they could hunt tigers in the Kraft jungle. We hurried to the back yard and found it had taken on a fierce, primitive look while we were busy in front. Grasses swayed hypnotically in the breeze, and jungle birds dipped and flashed with the grace of English sparrows and robin redbreasts. "Cut it," my wife said crisply. "We don't want this stuff going to seed, do we?"

"Why not?" I asked.

"On the other hand," she said, "spading it under to get organic matter in the soil might be a better . . ."

"I'll cut it," I said. "I'll phone some of the fellows, and we'll throw a safari party. You fix a few platters of whatever sandwiches you think my friends would enjoy, and put some beer on ice." Somewhere in the veldt I could hear the twins whooping it up as if they had just found the tiger. They had, though it answered to the name of Socks.

"All you need is a cutter and some elbow grease," my wife said. "I know your friends."

I borrowed a sickle from the twins' father. He had it all sharpened up and waiting for me, and it cut all right, but the work was slow and bendy. "You aren't making much of a dent," my wife said on a tour of inspection down a path I had hacked out. She borrowed the sickle and made a few swings with it. She was pretty good.

"Excellent for the figure," I said, stepping back out of harm's way and lighting a cigarette. "You seem to have a knack. I'll study your style."

"Why, there's nothing to it," she said, returning the

sickle. "It's sort of fun. Bend from the waist and make a game of it."

The fun kept me on the sofa most of the evening resting up, even though the sickle owner had come over and given me a hand after a while out of common humanity and a desire to recover his sons. He really was quite a guy, and when I limbered up again, he helped me rake up the hay and then loaned me his lawnmower to mow the stubble.

"Just as I thought," he said, observing the result. "You had a lawn under here all the time." True. After a few days of growth it put the pampered front lawn to shame. And it started something.

"You know," my neighbor said casually, "you could set up a badminton court here."

"I could?" I said.

"Wonderful muscle tonic," he said, and added that he'd install one on his own lawn except that his wife's lilacs were in the way. So was his wife, but he didn't go into that.

"Like to have a badminton court?" I asked my own wife. "Sampson next door says we have the perfect spot for one back there."

"That sounds like fun," she said. "We could give some badminton parties."

It was a prophetic remark. There is simply nothing like a jolly yard to get you known around the neighborhood, and in no time our yard began to pick up traffic.

People who had been just house numbers to us were suddenly Paul and Mary, Jack and Sally, Dave and Eagle-eye Marje.

And the twins' father (or Swatter Sampson, as he quickly became known) then got another idea. He supplied half the concrete blocks for an outdoor grill and helped me build it and taught me how to run it. The thing kicked up sociability so much more that we had to install an outdoor dart-board range to accommodate the new arrivals. We were speculating on a possible swimming pool when my wife and I were suddenly offered a deal on another house and took it.

As I see it now, our moving away was the hand of fate reaching out to save a young gardener from the paralyzing effects of a small and too-soon success. For the yard in the new house was a new challenge—in fact it was nothing but a four-inch piecrust of clay on top of a deepdish junk yard full of rusty automobile springs and surprises. And from this we staggered on to greater challenges:

A southern swamp some jesting builder had put a house on; a yard in Virginia with a glacial deposit of boulders as big as refrigerators in shallow graves; a California yard that sloped sharply up in back and tried to move into the house in wet weather; a farmhouse lawn in Missouri that attracted one-thousand-pound cows. . . . And there have been others, flinging down such challenges as salt water seeping up from mysterious depths, and underground-dwelling crawfish dotting the St. Augustine grass lawn with mud chimneys.

Wouldn't you think that somewhere along here there would be a burst of insight, like the comic-strip light bulb of inspiration above the character's head? You'd think so, and I'd think so, but fate doesn't think so. Only a few years ago I found myself in Mississippi with two acres of lawn to keep mowed with a small you-push-it rotary mower whose bearings were going merely because I had kept wondering what would happen if I cut just a little farther into the orchard and a little farther into the pecan grove each time I mowed, which was weekly over an eight-month season. The only way I could get the two acres off my back in the end was by selling the place to a man whose wife needed exercise.

Then there are these friends of ours, a couple familiar with the trouble a lawn can make, so when they bought a house of their own after renting places for a long time, the husband said he knew exactly what to do with the huge front yard. He called in a landscape artist and told him to scrape it clean of all the growth—grass, weeds, and scrubby shrubs—and replace this with four inches of clean sand. On the sand he was to plant some giant cacti, dump weathered slabs of wood and a few wagon wheels here and there, and spot some bleached cattle skulls. It looked so much like a desert, a neighborhood joker planted a "Last Chance for Gas" sign on it.

Well, they no sooner had it all fixed up than along

came a big rain, and it turned out the yard was about two feet lower than anything else around there. Maybe the landscape artist had been too arty. Anyway, a pond formed in their desert, and when it drained away into the ground, millions of seeds that had been snugly waiting under the sand sprouted. In no time the owner had to start mowing his desert. Funny thing is, he's got a better stand of grass on the sterile sand than he ever had on hauled-in topsoil.

Chapter 29

THE AMATEUR COMPETITION

THIS happens in New Orleans, usually in January: migrating robins pause to refresh themselves, and among the things they gobble are old ligustrum and pyracantha berries—so old they are fermenting. What happens next? Just what you'd expect. Those birds get drunk as lords on the high berries. They topple off branches. They lie on the ground in the parks. They stagger about, daring the New Orleans cats to put up their dukes. They are bug-eyed happy robins while it lasts, and they remind me of springtime gardeners.

The springtime gardener's fermenting berry is a seed catalog. It comes in January, too, and has the same intoxicating effect. And no wonder. Listen to this, will you?: "Tender, fine-textured skin and flesh at the eating stage provide delicately delicious flavor." That's not rainbow trout they're talking about—it's a squash. Squash! And how do you feel about parsnips? Hate them, eh? Hark to the missionary on parsnips: "Fine-grained, tender, sugary flesh of a pleasing delicate flavor." Whoops.

Quick—an order blank: "1 pkt parsnips." Or make it an ounce, so we won't run out of sugary flesh to go with pork tenderloin in the feasting time ahead.

You can't blame these springtime gardeners. The catalog is bigger than they are. Can't even blame those who never turn a spadeful of earth. I knew one such whose spring reading each year was catalogs from I guess about twenty seed houses and nurseries, some of them dealing in exotic, costly things. He didn't mind the cost, because he never bought anything. He lived in an apartment, and while he no doubt could have had a window box or two on the south side, he scorned window boxes. He was a big-garden man. An acre was little enough, he used to say, to provide a decent selection, and when I was planting an orchard once, he told me the best peach and plum varieties to get. He was right, too, though I had to find it out by buying the wrong varieties first on my own. I forgot to say that his wife put up with the stacks of catalogs—he saved them and had ceiling-high bookcases full of them, filed by years—on condition they keep right on living in the apartment.

Not every springtime gardener who doesn't garden at all has the excuse of no place to do it, though. In spite of their initial enthusiasm, some just never get down to digging, and there are two theories offered to account for this. One is that they wear themselves out, or at least grow sated, planning their gardens on paper. The other theory blames the catalogs by saying it's the decisions that paralyze the would-be gardeners. There's something to that decision business, especially with vegetables. If you want a pink zinnia you want a pink zinnia—not a red, white, or yellow one. But say you're trying to pick a simple little cucumber.

Well, here's one in the catalog called Ashley that's resistant, it says, to downy mildew. That must be good, eh? Who wants to eat downy mildew? And Ashley is dark green and stays well-shaped, crisp, and tender, says catalog. Good old Ashley. Let's order—

But wait. Here's one called Black Diamond that beats Ashley at bearing by nine whole days. Kind of sneaky of Ashley not to mention being such a slowpoke, wasn't it? Furthermore, catalog says Black Diamond is "refreshing and very tasty." Come to think of it, old Ashley ducked the question of taste completely too. Probably tastes like blotting paper. Well! Black Diamond it is, then—

Just a second. What's this about Improved Long Green being popular for both pickling and slicing? Nothing was said about pickling Black Diamond. Probably no darn good for pickling, and come to think of it, pickles are pretty tasty with a little cheese and a bottle of beer, slice or two of rye. So—let's make it Improved Long Gr——

Whup. Look here—catalog says this one called Marketer is extra fancy. You know that must be good. This is probably the gourmets' cucumber. . . . Uh, one moment. Here's one that won a bronze medal, Smoothie by name. Well, if it won a bronze medal, it obviously is better than any—*Wait a minute.* Here's one copped a *Gold* medal. Called Straight Eight. Catalog says it's a whitespine one, whatever that is, and symmetrical, deep color, highest quality. Certainly can't beat tha——But still . . . they don't call *it* extra fancy, like Marketer. Or mildew-resistant, like Ashley. And it's not as fast as Black Diamond. And what about pickling? And . . . oh, shucks.

Some gardeners are like a bride I knew who was so determined to master cooking that she made up her mind to work her way through her cookbook a recipe at a time until she had tried everything. When last heard from she was on intimate terms with seventy-five varieties of soup, and her husband gurgled when he danced. I know of no gardeners who have tried everything in a seed catalog, but it is a powerful temptation.[1]

On the other hand, I know an amateur gardener in Noel, Missouri, who sort of went to the other extreme and became a specialist on growing only spinach. It was the only thing she could grow, for some mystifying reason, but it she could grow by the tubful. Unfortunately her husband and daughter hated spinach and always had, and she wasn't so keen about it herself, but by then she had become the spinach queen of southwest Missouri, poor thing, and had to act as if she enjoyed the stuff.

[1] There is this about trying out different varieties of a plant— one of them may be exactly what your climate agrees with, and sometimes this is a variety the catalog is only mildly excited over.

Well, about these strictly springtime gardeners who do actually turn a clod. They're the worst of all. They're the amateur competition, compounded of enthusiasm and ignorance in equal parts. At the first little touch of spring, out dashes the springtime gardener, to scratch and harry a bit of ground in a frenzy of planting. The experienced old dogs of gardeners in the neighborhood know as well as they know their shoe size that it is too early to plant anything. May still be a frost. Even if there isn't weather's too cold to germinate seed. Even if seed should germinate, plants won't grow fast. Even if it warms up and they do grow fast, they—Even if they *do* grow fast—?

At this point something snaps, and the gardening veteran goes charging outdoors, gritting his teeth, to garden against all his better instincts. Because sometimes, once in a long while, the fool amateur is accidentally right. The earth is workable, the seeds sprout, the plants flourish. And he beats the pants off every veteran gardener in the neighborhood. You don't take a chance like that twice, friend.

Chapter 30

TOOLS—PETS AND PAINS

AS CHILDREN grow up, one of the worst things a gardening parent has to put up with is the gifts he gets from the little vipers on Father's Day, birthdays, and so on. If they would give him something practical—a barrel of compost, a day's weeding, back-ache cure—that'd be elegant, but they don't. They give him garden gadgets. Calling these tools would be frivolous. They are things that somebody who is spending all his time in a hermetically sealed room has designed on paper while laughing himself silly. The recipient often even has to ask what the thing is for. "Why, naturally to weed with, Pop," the poor man will be told of the bow-legged walking stick with a battery-powered light for night work that he has just unwrapped, and for fear of hurting anyone's feelings, he'll decide against asking which end you weed with.

As anyone—and certainly his own children—should know, Pop has his own favorite tool for weeding. As a matter of fact, the children do know it, and a lot of good that does. "Here's just the thing for him—a *whachama-callit* for weeds. He can finally throw away that worn-out old hoe he's been using a million years." He'd as soon throw away his liver. He'd be lost without the old hoe, whose blade is worn down to half its former width, which meets the earth at just the angle he likes, and which nobody else can use for ten minutes without walking bent over for the next three hours.

Or his pet tool may be a spade with a heft he likes, or a trowel that keeps its edge because years ago it was lost and got all rusty. At least that's what some people will swear is what makes steel hold an edge. I don't know if it's so, but I do know that the best ax I've ever had is pitted from the rust of years of neglect. I found it in the shed of a place we once bought, and when we moved five thousand miles away, I sawed off the handle and put the ax head in my suitcase among the socks and handker-chiefs.

As far as that goes, favorite tools usually are rusty and generally poor-looking. Before the psychiatrists get hold of this, I'll put in a simple two bits' worth and make a guess that a gardener's favorite tool looks terrible because he wants it handy all the time, so it gets more use and more weather than unfavorite ones.

You can imagine what happens when a favorite tool is missing. This is the kind of thing that can send the women and children fleeing into the streets while the old man boils all over the place hunting for the bent-handled little steel scratcher he can't cultivate the border beds with anything else but. A wife who will toss her man's pet old slippers and robe into the Goodwill truck would swoon if she found she had accidentally given away the toothless rake he uses to smooth seedbeds.

One gardener I know keeps a plastic squeeze bottle in his garden, filled with a liquid fertilizer. One squeeze per sprinkling can of water is exactly right, he has found. No further measuring needed, and no other squeeze bottle will possibly do. But the plastic bottle is getting old and brittle, and its squeeze is going, and the man's wife is waiting on the edge of her chair for the day it finally fails. That will be a black time, she knows, so she is planning to use it for something constructive, perhaps a weekend cram course in Yoga.

I don't want to leave the impression that only male gardeners have favorite tools, or are victims of the gadget. However, women don't make as much fuss about it. A woman whose favorite old tablespoon, invaluable for little transplantings, disappears, knows there are plenty more like it in the kitchen, darn it. Or she may mourn for a time the loss of a five-dollar, feather-light spade that doubled as an edger, but she can be cheered up by buying her a substitute. Twenty-five dollars' worth of nursery stock is an acceptable substitute.

My wife used to have a favorite tool that some people thought odd. It was a kind of plow, only instead of a horse in front, pulling, there she was in back, pushing.

One wife-power. This thing had three curved blades, and in front was a big wheel. A wheel hoe is what they call it, and its great advantage was speed. You could cultivate as fast as you could push, and have a heart attack at the end of each row.

About those garden-gadget gifts again—I knew a big family whose members were all gardeners, and one day one of them got a fool kind of gift gadget: a mole trap that they all could see wouldn't work on their brainy local moles.

Well, the one who got the gift palmed it off on another member of the family the next birthday that came up. Big joke. Then that one passed it along to the next birthday child, and so it went for a year or two, everybody getting hysterics each time the ridiculous thing was unwrapped.

Then one of the boys got married, and the current holder of the gadget gave it to the bride as a gag. She opened it, and everybody laughed—everybody but she. "Listen, these things work," she said. "My dad cleaned out every mole in his yard with one." That killed the laugh, especially later on, when it turned out the girl was absolutely right. The gadget actually did work. The incident impressed the family so strongly, it took two or three years before any of them really cared for their new in-law.

Chapter 31

GLAMOUR IN THE TOOL SHED

TO SIDETRACK a certain number of letters all beginning: "Listen, Kraft, you've got a nerve scoffing at garden gadgets," most of them from manufacturers of garden gadgets, I will admit there are useful ones as well as gift gadgets. The biggest difference is in the price. Pop might adore a $150 power post-hole digger, but a $4.95 hose nozzle he has no use for is more his children's speed. Consequently this other type of gadget is one the gardener must usually buy for himself, and the trouble is, he often does.

I'm not saying these things don't work. (For convenience's sake let's call them glamour gadgets, O.K.?) They'd better work, considering what they cost. What I'm saying is, they work in the wrong directions.

For instance, I know a man whose main gardening responsibility was to keep the brush trimmed along the driveway and fences of their rural home. He did it with a simple hand pruner and had time for his matchbook-cover collection, too. Then one day, don't ask me why,

he went and bought a thing with a kind of buzz saw on
one end of a steel stick and a little two-cycle gasoline
engine sitting in the middle. You held the other end,
started the engine, and you were in business. The gadget
went after brush like a Boy Scout after on old lady on a
curbstone. It really worked. So what's wrong with that?
Here's what's wrong: This brush-cutting man immediately became entranced with the gadget, babied it,
polished it, took it apart and learned all its bits and pieces
by heart. He had no time at all any more for his other
interests and not even very much for his wife. His brush
is trimmed beautifully, true, but it was all right before.

At that, he's in better shape than another fellow I
know. (By the way, this glamour gadget affliction is a
male disease. Women gardeners seem immune.) This
man had a few fruit trees he was always weeding around.
He had a theory it encouraged the roots to breathe. He
did this weeding with a mattock, and it helped keep him
in shape.

Then what did he do but loiter one day in the garden
department of a big store and become infatuated with a
power cultivator. Wonderful for keeping down weeds, the
salesman told him. I have nothing against power cultiva-
tors and wish I had had one a few years ago when I was
cultivating a half-acre garden of pure clay. The thing is,
though, what happened to this fruit-tree weeding man.
He became involved with this cultivator (which, incidentally, nearly shook his teeth loose with its astonishing

shimmy action), and since it did the fruit-tree job in about a tenth of the time it had taken him before, he felt frustrated. "I'm just getting started when I'm all finished," he complained to his wife. She suggested he do something constructive with his new leisure, such as learning to darn socks. However, he was a fellow without ambition, and he finally developed a nervous stomach and had to sell the machine at a disastrous price and go back to the mattock.

This power-cultivating thing gets to be a passion with some men. There was one who retired and bought a place in the South with five or six acres of flat, cleared land. Planted it in pecans. Next thing his wife knew, he'd bought a small riding tractor and a disk cultivator to go with it. Since he was careful and methodical, it took him three days to cultivate the entire plantation—a nice, satisfying parcel of work. One or two such cultivations a year are enough for most pecan growers, but this man reasoned that if one or two a year were good, twenty or thirty would be better. And that, actually and literally, is what he did. He called it "tractoring," and he tractored those poor little pecan trees every week the ground wasn't too wet to work.

The result was, it took them five years to make one year's growth. Pecans are shallow-rooted, and he kept slicing off their feeder roots nearest the surface. They never did get around to making any nuts during the time I knew them, and the only good thing I can say for the tractoring is that one year when a hurricane blew down a good many bearing pecans in the vicinity, the tractoring man's trees were too skinny for the wind to bother with.

With the glamour gadgets especially, there is the problem of borrowing. The man who lends his fancy tool is a rare bird, and one who lends it without running after the borrower with extra last-minute cautions and instructions and then holding his breath every time he hears it sputter, is almost unheard of. This leads, in the case of some men, to a semi-involuntary servitude. They lend themselves along with their glamour gadget. In that way they know at least that it won't be hurt by anybody else. Thus, a gardener so unlucky as to acquire an electric lawn edger or hedge trimmer may find himself edging lawns or trimming hedges of up to five gardens on either side of his, and sometimes across the street.

Just to keep things honest, I had better mention one case—the only one I know of—where a sort of glamour gadget was quite satisfactory. This happened to a woman gardener in Connecticut. The gadget—a fire-throwing thing to kill weeds—belonged to her husband. They lived in a nice rural neighborhood, and one day the woman heard a great clanking and rumbling out front and rushed to see. The noise was coming from a bulldozer making its way up their private road, which happened to be blocked just then by a huge and precious pile of manure the woman had managed to get for her herbaceous borders.

The bulldozer man was getting ready, obviously, to nudge it aside, and he told her he'd been hired to bulldoze an entry road on through to some acreage beyond—a disaster in our heroine's eyes. Without getting technical about it, this was one of those property-rights tangles of some years' standing where a smart operator sometimes finds a loophole in the law.

But being a woman, the gardener here did not fool around with the legal niceties. She dashed for the tool shed and returned clutching her husband's fancy weed burner. "Now, then," she said, leaping to the top of the manure pile, "you touch my manure with that thing, and whoosh!"

The bulldozer man didn't even stop to wonder if it was charged and ready. "My contract don't call for getting my fool head toasted off," he said, and backed all the way out. That ended the hanky-panky.

Mostly, though, the glamour gadgets are more apt to cause problems than to solve them. Speaking again of real estate, a real estate man I knew was so accustomed to this as a hazard of his business that he used to break out in spots when selling country property if the question of including power equipment in the deal came up. Once a sale of a $135,000 estate fell through because the owner, having made several other concessions, finally set his teeth and refused absolutely to throw in free a walking tractor and attachments. The buyer wouldn't budge either. Said he was entitled to a little lagniappe and didn't care to do business with tightwads.

"Liberally estimating," the real estate man told me, "the tractor and attachments were worth no more than five hundred dollars. But there's something about these wretched power tools that addles a man's reasoning." He sighed. "That would've been a sweet commission— six thousand seven hundred fifty dollars. I could have soaked six thousand away and had enough left for a compost grinder, power spray, and gang mower."